To:

_____

From:

_____

A Book for Dad

A Book for Dad

Rod Green

Michael O'Mara Books Limited

First published in Great Britain in 2010 by
Michael O'Mara Books Limited
9 Lion Yard
Tremadoc Road
London SW4 7NQ

A CIP catalogue record for this book is available from the British Library.

Papers used by Michael O'Mara Books Limited are natural, recyclable products
made from wood grown in sustainable forests. The manufacturing processes
conform to the environmental regulations of the country of origin.

ISBN: 978-1-84317-454-7

1 2 3 4 5 6 7 8 9 10

www.mombooks.com

Designed by Ana Bjezancevic

Typeset by K DESIGN, Somerset

Printed and bound in Great Britain by Clays Ltd, St Ives plc

To Bill Green and Witek Zukowski for being great dads

Contents

Introduction

DADS ARE STRANGE and wonderful creatures. They are one of the few things that absolutely everyone has in common (Mum is the other one that immediately springs to mind), yet every dad is totally different. They are a perplexing phenomenon; sometimes overwhelming, sometimes hands-off, sometimes your best friend, sometimes hard to get to know – and sometimes all of those in one man.

Light-hearted and full of fun, *A Book for Dad* is a celebration of fatherhood, presenting touching, inspirational real-life stories as well as laugh-out-loud ridiculous tales that will have Dad reminiscing about all the special times he has spent with his kids – and practical tips and advice for creating plenty more.

There are real legends of heroic fathers; historical yarns about daring deeds by fathers of previous eras; quotes from celebrity dads about their kids; stories of ordinary fathers; words of wisdom for first-time fathers; tips on being a modern dad; suggestions for great things to make and do with your children; dos and don'ts for dads; and a celebration of what makes dads so great.

Dad is the one for whom you find it most difficult to buy a present but you still desperately want to please – and thankfully this book is the ideal solution to that little problem. After all, how could any father fail to be delighted with something that so obviously declares your admiration for him?

The brand new dad

IT'S NOT DIFFICULT to father a child. Men have been doing so for quite some time now and, let's face it, if siring offspring were a tiresome task, then some bright spark would have found an effective way round it by now in order that men could spend more time doing important things like having a beer with their chums and watching football.

Being a *good* dad, on the other hand, isn't quite so straightforward. It takes a great deal of application, consideration, patience and effort, all starting long before the baby is actually born. The first step on the road to being a good dad is to look after the expectant mum. She might not always appreciate your efforts, and hormone-induced pregnancy mood swings might mean that she turns on you for no apparent reason, but it is a dad's job to give her all the support that she needs – even when she tells you to stay well clear because you're the idiot who got her into this state in the first place.

It's not easy waiting patiently for nine months to become a dad, but expectant fathers have so much to look forward to.

First-time dads' emergency kit

Anyone who is an old hand at bringing up a baby knows all the bits and pieces that they need to carry around with them. You will find yourself taking as much stuff with you when you pop out for a visit to show off your new offspring as you used to pack for a two-week holiday in the sun. There always seems to be something, though, that gets left behind.

Maybe the answer is to have a little emergency kit – a kind of survival pack for sleep-deprived, brain-addled first timers – that you always keep in the car. But what should you put in it? How about:

❖ A little toy similar to, preferably identical to, that favourite one your child delights in hurling out of the pram as soon as you're not looking. When the baby is screaming for it and it was last seen heading off at a gallop in the mouth of a delighted Labrador, you'll be glad you packed a replacement.

❖ Spare clothes. No matter how often you remind yourself that your baby has the capacity to poo, dribble or throw up on every item of clothing in its wardrobe, there will always be a time when you forget to bring a change.

❖ Nappies and baby wipes – the ones that you carefully laid out to bring with you have an incredibly annoying habit of not actually making it into the day bag that you packed.

❖ Baby food or formula milk powder ready to be pressed into service when the stuff you did bring with you ends up all over the floor.

❖ A spare feeding bottle. Even the toughest bottle that you regularly use can spring a leak at the wrong moment after it has been slammed into a table or chucked out of the pram for the umpteenth time.

❖ A blanket or shawl that you can use when the nice one that you wanted everyone to see your child cosily wrapped in is covered with regurgitated lunch.

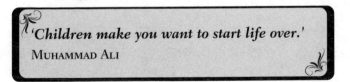

'Children make you want to start life over.'
MUHAMMAD ALI

❖ Spare contact lenses. Not for the baby, but for you. Babies have an uncanny knack of being able to insert a finger into your eye when you least expect it at precisely the right angle to dislodge a contact lens, which is then impossible to find on the grass in the park because you only have one fully functioning eye.

After a couple of excursions with baby, you will doubtless be able to refine this list, customizing it to suit whatever calamities you may have experienced. On the other hand, you might be one of the lucky few who never needs the emergency kit . . .

> 'You and I change, people change all through the months and years, but a photograph always remains the same. How nice to look at a photograph of mother or father taken many years ago. You see them as you remember them.'
> ALBERT EINSTEIN

The best laid plans

Martin took the idea of becoming a dad very seriously. He went with his wife, Susan, when she was having her scans at the hospital and, of course, had a lump in his throat and a tear in his eye when he saw the grainy image of his unborn child on the monitor. Being an organized sort of chap, he was also happy to be told the sex of his child, the doctor and nurse in attendance both agreeing that the image on the screen was a baby girl.

Back home, Martin began preparing for the baby's arrival. He cleared the small room that he had been using as a study so that it could become a nursery. He painted it pink and went shopping with Susan to buy the cutest little pink-and-flowery, girly baby clothes. He informed friends and relatives that they were having a baby girl. The little nursery room was soon a sea of pastel-pink rag dolls and teddies.

Then Susan went into labour and . . . gave birth to a fine, strong, healthy baby boy.

'They said at the hospital that they couldn't always be absolutely sure,' Martin admitted, 'and it didn't matter a bit. He is the most beautiful thing in the world and we are both incredibly proud of him. I suppose I'll have to repaint the nursery again, eventually . . .'

Advice for the first-time father

Before your little bundle of joy comes along, you have no idea just how irrevocably your life will change. The impact of such a tiny thing is so hard to predict that it will inevitably take you by surprise. There is the bewildering joy of seeing your own child gazing and gurgling at you, and your new-found obsession with their every move; and, of course, the less adorable sleepless nights and day-to-day childcare. While every couple has each other to turn to for support, it's always good to bear in mind the following . . .

❖ Talk to any of your male friends who have kids – especially ones who have had them recently. They'll be able to impart invaluable advice based on their own experience, and can offer much-needed support in those early days.

❖ Use all the resources you can, whether it's books, magazines or the internet, to help you feel more assured in what you're doing – you'll find plenty of chat forums and websites offering words of wisdom. When it comes to your baby's health, however, take no chances and make sure you consult your own GP.

❖ Make sure you share the responsibility of getting up during the night equally. If Mum wants to breastfeed you can still get up with her so she doesn't feel like

she's the only one having to get out of bed through
the night.

❖ Be flexible. That clockwork routine you had before
Junior came along is simply unrealistic now. Again,
taking turns with your partner and figuring out
between you who has plans or work that need to be
prioritized will help. You will have to sacrifice a great
deal of your leisure time, but it's worth it!

❖ *Relax* and enjoy it! Being a father is an unforgettable
and miraculous experience, the most amazing
rollercoaster ride of your life. The time will fly
quicker than you know so make sure you make the
most of every minute.

Bonding with baby

> 'Take comfort from the fact that whatever
> you do in any fathering situation has a fifty
> per cent chance of being right.'
> BILL COSBY

Although connecting with your newborn is pretty
instinctive, that doesn't mean there aren't things you
can do to strengthen that bond further. Things are

changing rapidly in order to recognize the shared responsibility of parenting, the difference between maternity and paternity leave does mean that as a dad you will probably have less time with your child, so it's important that when you are home you make the best use of your time with your partner and kid(s).

Aside from splitting the childcare duties, such as changing nappies, bath time, putting baby to bed and getting up in the night, there are lots of ways you can bond with your baby . . .

❖ Touch is vitally important, especially in those early days, so simply playing with children and holding them helps strengthen the attachment.

❖ Speaking or singing in a soft voice is especially reassuring for them, and can also help them begin to understand basic communication.

❖ Lots of eye contact is beneficial too, as babies are quick to pick up facial signals.

❖ More than anything, however, showing your baby love and care and giving it your time and attention when you are at home are the best ways to start a happy lifelong relationship with your child.

Internet baby

Guys love playing with gadgets and they don't give up their boys' toys just because they're about to become dads. The amount of time that Leroy spent phoning, texting or browsing the internet using his mobile was a constant source of annoyance for Emma. After all, when a girl's about to give birth to a baby, she likes to feel that she is the centre of attention and doesn't appreciate competition from technology.

Emma had decided that she wanted to have her baby at home and the couple were visited regularly by their midwife. The midwife had made her final visit of the day when Emma began to experience contractions that were so powerful and came so quickly that they knew the baby was about to be born.

Leroy called the midwife, who immediately headed back to their house, but it was clear that she wasn't going to make it in time. Neither did they have time to get Emma to a hospital, and the thought of the baby being born somewhere along the way filled both parents with dread.

So Leroy picked up his trusty mobile and Googled 'how to deliver a baby'. He carefully followed the instructions that he found on the internet, safely delivering their healthy, 6lb 11oz daughter Mahalia.

When the midwife arrived she congratulated Leroy on having done such a good job and Emma has vowed never to chastise Leroy for messing around with his phone ever again!

'It is a wise father that knows his own child.'
WILLIAM SHAKESPEARE

Modern dads cope best

··

THERE ARE THE most wonderful things that you will discover and share being a modern dad, and there are also some less than enviable experiences that you will have to go through.

You may think of yourself as a sophisticated and intelligent grown-up, able to hold your own when it comes to a heated debate in the workplace; you may think you can still be counted on to put in a good performance on the football pitch; you may have attended all of the antenatal classes, but you are still no match for the stamina and unpredictability of a new baby.

Fortunately, children lose most of their unpredictable baby ways as they grow older . . . though they then learn all sorts of new ones. None of these endearing traits, however, will stop you from feeling like the world's proudest dad.

Dos and don'ts for dads: at the cinema

❖ **Do** pay for a handful of your child's friends to join her/him on a trip to the cinema as a birthday treat. Even if you take them all for a pizza afterwards, it works out less expensive than a big party and your house doesn't get wrecked.

❖ **Do** make sure that all of the kids have been to the loo before you settle down to watch the movie.

❖ **Do** think carefully about the kind of movie you take them to. Other parents won't thank you if the movie gives their kids nightmares for weeks.

❖ **Do** buy tickets that allow all of your party to sit together. If a couple are sitting apart from the main group, they may be upset about it, or, knowing they are out of your reach, use it as an excuse to try out their very worst behaviour.

❖ **Don't** let the little horrors have lots of sugar-heavy fizzy drinks and toxic sweets – they'll all be going nuts before the trailers have finished.

❖ **Don't** close your eyes – even for a second – the children will be watching. The cinema is warm and dark. You are in a comfortable chair. You will wake up two hours later thinking you've gone blind and deaf. Ticket stubs slipped inside your glasses and popcorn in your ears can do that to a man.

Quick-thinking dad

Every child loves to go out in the park after a rainy spell and splash about in puddles. It's what wellies were made for, after all. For Leona Baxter, however, splashing in a puddle would have cost her her life had it not been for the speedy thinking of her dad, RAF Sergeant Mark Baxter. It was September 2008 and the three-year-old was having fun in a play area in a local park, jumping in puddles with her six-year-old sister and their dog, Brophy.

The kids' parents watched as Leona appeared to fall over. They expected her to get up, soaking wet, but she simply disappeared. Mark rushed over to the puddle, thinking he could just lift her out of the water, but she wasn't there, and when he stuck his hand in the water, it went down, and down, and down. Then he noticed a kind of whirlpool in the puddle and when Brophy came splashing over, the dog also disappeared beneath the water. By now, Mark was lying full stretch and, reaching down with one arm, could feel nothing but swirling,

'Being a dad is the new black.'
LAURENCE LLEWELYN-BOWEN

fast-moving water. Suddenly, he touched what felt like a manhole cover. Flood water from the heavy rain had forced the cover off a storm drain. His daughter had gone underwater and underground.

Mark quickly realized that the drain had to lead to the River Weir, about two hundred feet away across the park. He covered the distance at breakneck pace and spotted Leona floating in the water. He jumped straight in, the swollen river water reaching his shoulders. When he hauled Leona from the water she was perfectly still and not breathing. Patting her on the back as he waded his way back to the river bank, Mark handed Leona to his wife, and was relieved to hear Leona cough and retch as he dragged himself out of the river. She was alive and, miraculously, suffered no more than a few cuts and bruises – and a nasty shock. Sadly, Brophy was never seen again.

Second half snooze

It was David's proudest moment when he took his six-year-old son, Robert, to his first football match. He had been a fan for years and turned out to watch all of his team's home matches. He always met up with his old chums sitting in the grandstand and he couldn't wait for Robert to join him. It would be an experience that they could share together for years to come.

When the afternoon of the big game came round, they took their seats to watch the action, well wrapped up against the cold winter weather. Little Robert was fascinated by the carnival atmosphere in the stadium. He stood on his seat to get a better view of the match and howled with delight when, as the daylight started to fail, the massive stadium floodlights were switched on.

By half time Robert was still bouncing around with excitement then, following a cup of his favourite hot chocolate that David had brought in a thermos flask, he snuggled in to keep warm and watch the second half. Dad, of course, was happy to have his son cuddled up close and made Robert as comfortable as he possibly could – big mistake. When the final whistle went and everyone stood up to leave, Robert stumbled to his feet.

'Who won?' he asked. Then, more annoyed, 'And why did you let me fall asleep?!' Robert was furious with his dad all the way home, more so when he realized that David found it funny. The whole experience had been just a little too much for the six-year-old, but luckily he forgave his dad, and it wouldn't be the last time that they went to watch a big game together.

Tips on being a modern dad

Tip 1: Be there from the start to the finish. Being a father is a role that never ends. You don't get to choose when to opt in and out of your child's life, but you'll find that you want to be there for them through thick and thin.

Tip 2: Work as a team with your partner. No man (or woman) is an island, and the only way to make parenting as stress free as possible is to work together, not only sharing the burden of daily duties, but making sure you never stop communicating with each other.

Tip 3: Be generous with your time. Gone are the days of Dad being a distant figure who plays a far less active role in his child's life than its mother. But working men and women still need to remind themselves every now and then to put time aside every day when their sole attention is on their child.

'By the time a man realizes that maybe his father was right, he usually has a son who thinks he's wrong.'
CHARLES WADSWORTH

Tip 4: Be a family (eat together, go out together and so on). As the world moves at a seemingly ever-increasing pace, it can be hard to find time to spend together as a family on a regular basis. Regardless of whether you are a couple or a single-parent family, it is important to create the feeling of being a unit. Simple things like sitting down at the table together for meals, or going out for a walk together can strengthen the family bond and give your child a greater feeling of security.

Tip 5: Show affection as well as authority. It can be easy to lose patience with young kids, particularly if you're a first-time dad. Children simply aren't as easy to control or predict as adults. As a result you do have to be firm in your discipline, but always ensure that they know this stems from your love for them, rather than anger.

Tip 6: Lead by example. Why would your child listen to you when told not to throw litter on the street if they have seen you doing it? It is essential that your children see you putting into practice what you preach, or your behaviour will seem unfair to them and they will be far less likely to do what they are told.

Tip 7: Let your child be their own person. It's perfectly natural for parents to have dreams for their child's future. But there does have to come a point at which you accept and cherish *their* dreams above your own – such as not wanting them to be the Prime Minister when they want to be a schoolteacher. Putting pressure on your child to be something they're not will only cause resentment in the long run.

Tip 8: Accept that you won't always be in control. Even the most organized, efficient man in the world will find himself flummoxed in the face of fatherhood. Although you can prepare yourself with advice from the very best resources, there are certain things that only experience can teach you. Try to go with the flow, and accept that things won't always go to plan.

Tip 9: Make sure you have one-to-one time with your partner. While giving as much time as you can to your child is vital, it is equally important to remember that as well as being parents you are also the two individuals you were before you started this exciting venture. It is far better for a child to see its parents relaxed and happy rather than permanently frazzled.

Tip 10: It's OK to be wrong. It can be a strange burden, having a child unquestionably accepting your version of the world, and parents often feel that they have to have an answer to everything. However, it's OK to let your child know if you don't know the answer to their question, or if you have got something wrong. Understanding that their parents and elders aren't perfect can take away some of the pressure for kids in those tricky early school years.

Nappy expert

James and Lydia attended antenatal classes together. At one of the classes a young mum who had recently given birth came along to show all of the couples exactly what a brand new baby looked like. The baby boy behaved beautifully, was quiet and gurgled on cue as everyone in the class crowded round to admire him.

The class had been discussing the pros and cons of modern disposable nappies as opposed to the more old-fashioned towelling type. Disposables were not considered to be 'green', because they are not generally good for recycling, while towelling nappies can be cleaned and re-used. This means more work for the parents, of course, and towelling nappies are also notoriously difficult to fold and wrap around a squirming infant.

There was a distinct lack of volunteers, therefore, when the new mum offered everyone the opportunity to change her baby's towelling nappy. However, then James stepped forward. He gently laid the baby down on a changing mat on the floor, removed the dirty nappy and dropped it in the nappy bucket that had been provided, then expertly cleaned the little lad, applied the nappy cream and had him safely trussed up in a clean nappy in no time at all.

'Well done, James,' said the midwife, suitably impressed. 'You handled that like a pro.'

'Yes,' sighed Lydia. 'He's been practising on the dog.'

It's a dad thing

A DAD IS expected to be able to do many things, from playing football and giving rides on his back to juggling and building Lego (not always at the same time). A dad won't always be able to join in with everything that his kids want to do and there will come a time when he has to take a step back to let the kids cope all on their own. As they grow older, the kids won't want Dad there when they're hanging out with their friends. They certainly won't want him sitting next to them at the cinema when they're on that all-important first date.

Dads go from being the one that every son wants to be like, the one that every daughter adores, to being the most embarrassingly uncool creature on the planet in the space of just a few short years. Until then, however, he is the top dog and absolutely nothing beats doing things with Dad.

The biggest 'dad thing' of all is feeling uncontrollably proud of his kids – it is the one thing that is absolutely guaranteed to bring a lump to any father's throat and send a tear rolling down his cheek: yes, tears of pride are most definitely a 'dad thing'. Here are some stories, of famous dads and their touching moments of pride and joy in their offspring.

Dad salutes you

Vinnie Jones is never described as anything other than a hard man. Famous for his aggression, strength and fitness on the football pitch, when his career as a professional footballer had come to an end, he kicked off his Hollywood movie career with the role of tough guy Big Chris in Guy Ritchie's *Lock, Stock and Two Smoking Barrels*.

Born the son of a gamekeeper, Vinnie was brought up in a macho environment, was familiar with guns

> 'When my father ran up the stairs and looked at his newborn son, he quipped, "He looks like a fat little Dutchman but, who knows, he might grow up to be president some day."'
> RONALD REAGAN

> *'Getting a burp out of your little thing is probably the greatest satisfaction I've come across. It's truly one of life's most satisfying moments.'*
> BRAD PITT

from an early age and grew up enjoying an outdoors life of hunting, shooting and fishing.

All of that gave Vinnie's son, Aaron, a lot to live up to. Rather than try to emulate his father's career in any way, however, Aaron decided to strike out on his own and joined the army. Vinnie flew over from his Los Angeles home to be at Aaron's passing out parade in Harrogate, North Yorkshire in 2008, saying 'I am very proud of him. It has been a very emotional experience.'

And the famous tough guy admitted to being more than a little concerned about Aaron's posting to Afghanistan with the Household Cavalry in 2010, although the proud dad had no doubt that his son could cope, declaring Aaron to be 'identical to me'. He did admit, however, that his son was now far fitter than him!

Top ten TV dads

The daddy	The show	The kids
1. Homer Simpson	*The Simpsons*	Bart, Lisa, Maggie
2. Ross Geller	*Friends*	Ben, Emma
3. Peter Griffin	*Family Guy*	Chris, Meg, Stewie
4. John Walton	*The Waltons*	John, Jason, Mary Ellen, Erin, Ben, Jim-Bob, Elizabeth
5. The Doctor	*Doctor Who*	Jenny
6. Martin Crane	*Frasier*	Frasier, Niles
7. Jack Bauer	*24*	Kim
8. Hal Wilkerson	*Malcolm in the Middle*	Francis, Reese, Malcolm, Dewey, Jamie
9. Fred Flintstone	*The Flintstones*	Pebbles
10. Dr Cliff Huxtable	*The Cosby Show*	Sondra, Denise, Theodore, Vanessa, Rudy

The perfect role

It's a lucky son or daughter who can properly share the experience of working alongside their dad. That's just what Will Smith's son, Jaden, did when Will made the movie *The Pursuit of Happyness* in 2006. In fact, according to Will, Jaden, then aged eight, didn't simply take a role in the movie, he put in a performance that forced his dad to pull out all the stops, leading to him being nominated for the Academy Award for Best Actor.

Jaden kept Dad on his toes, simply by doing what came naturally. In one scene shared by father and son, Will's nose started to run just as he delivered the line 'I'm a good Poppa'. 'I thought, "Damn it! The take's ruined!"' said Will. 'But Jaden reached up, wiped my nose and said: "You're a good Poppa."'

Will claimed that Jaden's thoroughly natural approach forced him to change his style, bringing forth one of his best ever performances. Jaden did his dad proud by winning the award for Breakthrough Performance at the 2007 MTV Movie Awards.

'Who I am as a father is far more important to me than the public perception.'
BRUCE WILLIS

What's in a name?

When your dad's a famous actor, you might be forgiven for taking full advantage of the family name but, to her father's pride, pop songstress Lily Allen refused to take the easy option – and instead took on various jobs including working in a flower shop to make ends meet, before finding success and a record deal by posting her music on MySpace. Now the tables are turned and it's Lily's turn in the limelight. Her father Keith joked, 'I've got an autobiography coming out and I'm going to call it "By Lily Allen's Dad", 'cause she's more famous than me.'

> 'The words that a father speaks to his children in the privacy of home are not heard by the world, but, as in whispering-galleries, they are clearly heard at the end and by posterity.'
> JEAN PAUL RICHTER, GERMAN AUTHOR

Keeping up with the kids

Comedian and actor Les Dennis was overjoyed to become a new dad at the age of fifty-four when his fiancée (now his wife), Claire, gave birth to Eleanor in 2008. Les was happy to do his share of nappy changing and baby chores, pointing out that he was an 'old hand', with a son, Philip, from a previous marriage.

Les's showbiz career had meant that he had been forced to spend more time away from baby Philip than he would have liked, but he still learned the basics of looking after a baby; skills that, once learned, are never forgotten. Philip, however, had been born twenty-eight years before the arrival of Eleanor and there was speculation in the press about how well Les would cope with the sleepless nights and exhausting routines associated with a new baby.

Then, when he was spotted shopping near his London home looking rather tired and bleary-eyed, it was assumed that he was not dealing well with being a dad. Nothing could have been further from the truth.

Les explained that he and Philip, along with a few friends, had 'had a few drinks' and 'a very late night out' celebrating the arrival of Eleanor. Looking after his daughter obviously wasn't quite as taxing for Les as keeping up with his son!

My dad's a pirate

Ask a random selection of eight-year-olds what their dads do and more than a few will tell you that 'he works in an office' or 'he works in a shop', but not many will tell you 'he's a pirate'. However, when Lily-Rose was taken ill and rushed into Great Ormond Street Hospital in London, she could have been forgiven for telling everyone that her dad was a pirate, and he proved it when he came for a visit. Lily-Rose, you see, is Johnny Depp's daughter, and Johnny Depp, as everyone knows, is Captain Jack Sparrow from *Pirates of the Caribbean*.

Johnny was filming *Sweeney Todd* at Pinewood Studios in Buckinghamshire while his partner, Vanessa Paradis, looked after Lily-Rose and her little brother, John, at a rented house in Richmond, Surrey, in March 2007. Lily-Rose unfortunately contracted an E.coli infection and, as she became increasingly unwell, she was rushed to Great Ormond Street. Her condition became critical and *Sweeney Todd* director Tim Burton halted the filming to allow Johnny to be with his family.

Lily-Rose battled through a desperate illness, but the staff at Great Ormond Street never gave up the fight to save her. After nine days, she was well enough to leave the hospital. Johnny described Great Ormond Street as 'terrific – a great hospital' and nine months later invited some of the doctors and nurses who had treated Lily-Rose to the VIP party at the London première of *Sweeney Todd*.

Prior to that, however, Johnny had arranged a special secret return visit to Great Ormond Street in November 2007. He had his Captain Jack Sparrow costume flown over from California to London and spent four hours at the hospital dressed as Captain Jack, telling stories to the children.

The grateful dad also donated £1 million to the hospital, although there is no truth in the rumour that it was delivered in a treasure chest filled with gold doubloons . . .

> *'Once I had my first hit, Dad started to introduce himself as Nancy Sinatra's father!'*
> NANCY SINATRA

The rebel

Rebelling against your parents is a natural thing for all children to do at some point in their lives, but it becomes more difficult if your parents have never left their rebellious youth behind and have never settled down into a conventional lifestyle.

Harry Gilliam, son of Monty Python animation guru and film director Terry Gilliam, is now in his twenties, but when he was a schoolboy his dad had the look of a disreputable hippy, all hair, occasional beard, beads, baggy shirts and jeans. How do you rebel against someone who is himself such a rebel?

The answer for Harry was to insist on dressing in a smart blazer and flannels and carry a briefcase to school. He would deliberately adopt a look that was the exact opposite of his father's. When he was a little older and embarking on a modelling career, Harry was rejected by one modelling agency because his hair was far too long to be trendy. He had grown long hair because his dad had had his cut short! Despite their differences, Harry and Terry remain the best of friends.

Father's Day

DADS WILL ALWAYS make out that Father's Day ranks way below Mother's Day in the league table of the most important days of the year. They will always lead you to believe that they don't like all the attention brought on by a special day; that they're really not hugely excited about the prospect of receiving a badly wrapped novelty soap-on-a-rope or yet another 'World's Greatest Dad' coffee mug. It is, of course, all boys' talk and bluster. Dads would be mortified if Father's Day were suddenly to be struck from the calendar. After all, the day for celebrating our fathers has been with us now for a whole century.

> *'My mother gave me my drive, but my father gave me my dreams.'*
> LIZA MINNELLI

Where it all began

The very first celebration of fatherhood is, unsurprisingly, disputed. As far back as nearly four thousand years ago a boy called Elmesu carved a message to his father on a tablet of clay, wishing him good health and a long life – which was found in the ruins of Babylon.

In Catholic countries, most notably Spain, Father's Day is traditionally celebrated on St Joseph's Day (19 March). However, the modern, secular celebration of Father's Day is more commonly attributed either to Grace Golden Clayton of West Virginia, who suggested that three hundred and fifty men who had died in a lethal explosion be commemorated in this way on 5 July, 1908, or to a lady called Sonora Smart Dodd.

A twenty-eight-year-old American woman, Sonora listened to a church service on Mothering Sunday and decided that something needed to be done for fathers, too. Married with a young son, Sonora appreciated the role of dad in child rearing more than most at that time. Her mother had died giving birth to her sixth child when Sonora was just sixteen, so Sonora's father, William Smart, shouldered the heavy responsibility of bringing up the new baby and his five other children alone, while also managing the family farm. As a new parent herself, Sonora had come to realize just how much hard work and sacrifice had been required of her father.

Sonora first approached the local church community where she lived in Spokane, Washington, with the idea of establishing a Father's Day celebration. As a tribute to her own father, she suggested his birthday (6 June) as the date for Father's Day, but the church authorities decided to go for the third Sunday in June instead. The first Father's Day celebration, therefore, took place on 19 June, 1910.

The idea didn't catch on straight away. Some derided Father's Day as a silly notion dreamt up purely for commercial exploitation and, although President Woodrow Wilson attended Father's Day services in Spokane in 1916 and President Calvin Coolidge gave the idea his support in 1924, it was to take more than forty years for Father's Day to receive official presidential approval. In 1966 Lyndon Johnson signed a proclamation declaring the third Sunday in June to be Father's Day.

> *'Small boy's definition of Father's Day: it's just like Mother's Day only you don't spend so much.'*
> ANONYMOUS

A global celebration

❖ More than fifty countries around the world, including the United Kingdom, have followed America's example to establish Father's Day on the third Sunday in June, while others, like Austria and Belgium, have it on the second Sunday.

❖ Still more countries have adopted dates throughout almost every month of the year, with Australia and New Zealand celebrating in September, while Bulgarians have their Father's Day on Boxing Day (26 December).

❖ In Germany, Ascension Day, which is the Thursday forty days after Easter, is a federal holiday and has developed into a Father's Day with a difference. In various parts of the country, it is known as *Vatertag* (Father's Day), *Männertag* (Men's Day) or *Herrentag* (Gentlemen's Day). One traditional German method of celebrating Father's Day is for groups of men to go hiking in the countryside, pulling behind them wooden trolleys or dog carts stacked with essential supplies for the outing – mainly copious quantities of beer and sausage. That beats smiling gratefully as you unwrap your brand new soap-on-a-rope any day!

❖ Roses are the official flower of Father's Day in a number of countries, apparently following Sonora Smart Dodd's lead after she was said to choose this flower for the day of celebration. You should wear red if your dad is alive, and white if your father is deceased.

❖ Father's Day in Thailand falls on 5 December, the king's birthday. For the celebrations the Thai people dress in yellow as a gesture of respect for the king.

❖ Argentina celebrates Father's Day on the third Sunday of June, but there have been various attempts to change it to coincide with the day that José de San Martín – the Argentine general known as the 'Father' of the Argentinians for helping bring about independence from Spain – became a father.

❖ In 2009 an estimated ninety-five million Father's Day cards were given in America.

❖ The first official Father's Day to be celebrated in Iceland was in November 2006, thanks to the approval of the social minister of the country.

Top ten dad records

The hit	The rocker
1. Daddy Cool	Boney M
2. Don't Cry Daddy	Elvis Presley
3. My Father's Eyes	Eric Clapton
4. My Dad's Gone Crazy	Eminem
5. Father to Son	Phil Collins
6. Dance with My Father	Luther Vandross
7. Papa Don't Preach	Madonna
8. My Father's House	Bruce Springsteen
9. Father and Daughter	Paul Simon
10. Son of My Father	Chicory Tip

Things for kids to do for Dad on Father's Day

1. Get him a thoughtful present and card.

2. Make him breakfast in bed – it's not just mums who appreciate this!

3. Clean his car – but take special care to use the right cleaning equipment so you don't damage any of its upholstery. The idea is to save him time, not cost him money in repairs!

4. Take part in one of his hobbies – hiking, watching the footie, fishing, rock climbing and so on.

5. Watch his favourite film together.

6. If you're old enough to drive, take him out for a spin in the country and go for a pub lunch.

7. Make a film of you (and your siblings if you have any) talking about your favourite times with him and why he means so much to you.

8. Cook him his favourite meal (hopefully for your sake it's not an elaborate, slow-cooked tagine). If he doesn't really have one just go for a classic family meal, like a roast, or if it's sunny have a barbeque – something that involves plenty of interaction between you all that will make him feel like you're making a special effort for him, without embarrassing him by making too much of a fuss.

....

9. If he's into sport, get the whole family tickets to his team's next match.

....

10. Help him tidy his shed.

....

11. Give him a hug – it costs nothing but it'll mean the world.

....

Clever Dad

Having a new baby in the house is a difficult time for kids, and when singer and actress Cher was a little girl, things were no different. She remembers the day that her baby sister, Georganne, was brought home from hospital and immediately captured everyone's attention. Suddenly Cher had gone from being the apple of everyone's eye to feeling like nobody even knew she existed. She was in her room, escaping from all the fuss, when her dad came in to have a chat. He asked her what she thought of her baby sister and Cher replied that she hadn't seen much of Georganne at all because so many other people had been fussing around her.

Cher describes in her book *The First Time*, how her dad said that he knew exactly how she felt and then whispered, 'Let's go in and kidnap her.' They sneaked Georganne into Cher's room and settled her on Cher's bed, with dad explaining that babies didn't really do much of interest but recommending that they 'keep her at least till she grows some hair.'

'My father was really smart about things like that,' said Cher. 'I loved him more than he could ever know.'

Holy Father's Day

It's always nice in church during the special service on Mothering Sunday when children are given the job of seeking out all the mums in the congregation to present them with a small gift, generally a posy of flowers, just to make sure that they feel appreciated and to say, 'Thanks for being a great mum.'

You can't really 'say it with flowers' when it comes to Father's Day but, to make sure that dads didn't feel left out, in 2009 St Stephen's Church in Barbourne, Worcester, decided that the dads in the congregation should also be given a blessing gift. Mums always like flowers, of course, but what kind of gift would be best for dads? After thinking about it for at least a second or two, they settled on . . . a bottle of beer. Some might think that it was inappropriate for the church to be handing out beer as part of their 'Fathering Sunday' service but, as the Bishop of Worcester pointed out, 'We give wine away every Sunday, so giving away beer could be said to be going downmarket, but it's an attempt to speak of God's generosity.'

It was also, of course, an attempt to attract men into the church on Father's Day and other churches tried similar ruses. In Amersham, one church held a hog roast outside to tempt men towards the front door, and a church in Nottingham handed out bacon rolls to men as they arrived on Father's Day.

The bank of Dad

THERE'S AN OLD saying that describes a dad as a man who has photos in his wallet where his beer money used to be. Kids are, without doubt, a serious drain on Dad's finances (and Mum's, as well, of course) and you can't charge them interest or late repayment fees. Your reward comes instead with every smile, every hug, every moment you spend with your children as they grow up. But your kids don't just need you to be a human cash point. They need you as a role model, an authority figure, a life coach and a free taxi service.

Remember, however, that everything you do for your kids ultimately goes towards teaching them how to be more independent and how to live their own lives successfully. Your time with them as their protector will be gone before you know it, but even once they have struck out on their own, it's always Dad they will turn to when they really need help. That help needn't mean that you have to start dipping into your life savings, either – your kids won't always bank with you, but they will always bank on you.

51

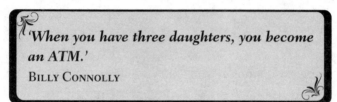

'*When you have three daughters, you become an ATM.*'
BILLY CONNOLLY

Things children should never do

....

1. Admit that your part-time job pays quite well and you don't need a handout.
....
2. Leave any party evidence after Dad's weekend away with Mum.
....
3. Turn your music up full blast when he shouts, 'Hey! That music's not loud enough, can you crank it up a bit?'
....
4. Before you've started shaving yourself, try out his aftershave for a laugh.
....
5. Reveal that your vocabulary is as bad as . . . um . . . like, whatever, yeah?
....
6. Offer to show him your new tattoo.
....
7. Give a truthful answer when he's angry and yells, 'Do I *look* stupid?'
....
8. Lose his TV remote.
....

Charitable children

Can you make money from your children? It might be nice to think that all of the pocket money, the football club fees, the ballet lessons, the tennis lessons, the school trips and the countless other expenses that burn up Dad's beer money could be recouped by introducing your children to the concept of 'earning their keep'. That's really not what being a dad is all about, though, is it?

On the other hand, Brad Pitt is a dad who knows all about how best to make millions from his kids. In 2006, Brad and partner Angelina Jolie sold the rights to the first photographs of their daughter Shiloh for $4.1 million in North America and $3.5 million internationally. They followed that up in 2008 with a massive $14 million for images of their twins Knox and Vivienne. While other celebrities were going to great lengths to keep their children *out* of the limelight, Brad and Angelina appeared to be doing precisely the opposite.

There was, however, method to this apparent madness. The press would eventually have 'sneaked' unofficial photographs of the youngsters for nothing; so instead, by selling the rights, Brad and Angelina ensured all of the money that was earned went to charitable organizations. The millions raised by the photographs of the twins went to the Jolie-Pitt Foundation, which donates many millions of dollars every year to charities all over the world. In previous years, the couple had also been known for donating millions to worthy causes at home and abroad. Their motives in offering their children up to the photographers' lenses are, therefore, beyond reproach.

It's a date!

Dads soon become accustomed to the hard-earned cash that they used to invest in important things like beer and football being diverted towards their children, and no true dad ever baulks at that. Providing for your kids is part of being a dad, after all.

Some dads, however, find the strangest ways to raise money for the benefit of their children. One group of dads from Kent decided to do a bit of fundraising for a local children's hospital that had, at some stage, looked after their kids. The money they made went to a very worthwhile charity that had been helping to provide essential equipment such as monitors, sterilizers and even beds for parents who had to stay overnight at the local hospital.

So how did they help to raise some cash (and a few smiles)? They took their cue from the hit movie *Calendar Girls* and stripped off as Calendar Dads! It was all done in the best possible taste and with great good humour and, while all of the money from calendar sales went to the charity, the dads' personal assets were kept cunningly concealed.

Teach your kids about money

You can't really blame your children for not understanding that money doesn't grow on trees when they're rarely taught how money works in the first place. So help yourself by teaching them a basic grasp of where your money comes from, how banks look after it, and the concept of interest rates as a bonus if you save money. These simple ideas, learnt early on, can give them an incentive to want to save more than they splurge in later life. It's not a guarantee of course, but you don't lose anything by trying, and you'll certainly lose more money by not trying! Here are some simple suggestions to get you started:

❖ **Buy your child a piggy bank.** It's a simple and fun way of teaching children how to save and really does get the message across that if you look after the pennies the pounds look after themselves.

❖ **Only give pocket money in return for completed chores.** Giving children money every week simply for being your children isn't a good way of teaching them its value. If you reward them for doing tasks such as the washing up every night for a week, or hoovering the carpet, or making the beds, they will understand the basic principle that money is something you earn, not something you have a right to.

❖ **Open a savings account for them.** When they are old enough to do jobs such as babysitting or a newspaper round, teach them the benefit of putting a certain amount of each pay packet into savings. It's never too early to set up an account for a child, though do keep control of access to it until they are old enough to be responsible for how they spend it.

❖ **With older children you can teach them how to keep a budget**, maybe buying them an attractively-covered book to keep a note of their accounts. It won't be easy trying to get a teenager to have the discipline to do this, but if you show them early enough you are at least planting a seed for later life.

'*A truly rich man is one whose children run into his arms when his hands are empty.*'
ANONYMOUS

Tough love

Every dad likes to lay down a few ground rules to try to keep his kids on the straight-and-narrow, and the rules can include making it clear when your child's overdraft at the Bank of Dad will finally be terminated. Reaching that fateful day is, no doubt, a painful experience for some, but actress Gwyneth Paltrow accepted it as part of moving on.

Gwyneth's father, Bruce Paltrow, was a successful producer/director who had never been reluctant to provide for his daughter. They visited Paris together when Gwyneth was just ten years old, Dad explaining that he wanted his daughter to see the city for the first time with a man whom she could be absolutely sure would love her forever. Dad made sure that Gwyneth had a good education but warned her that when she left university, she would have to pay her own way.

When Gwyneth dropped out of the University of California, Bruce was as good as his word. 'He didn't give me any money,' Gwyneth explained in an interview with *The Times*. 'I really struggled, and I waitressed and bought cigarettes out of tips and tried to get to auditions with no gas.'

Gwyneth accepted that she had to make her own way in life and was glad that she didn't have the safety blanket of a trust fund to fall back on. As far as she was concerned, instead of money, her dad had given her the drive and determination to succeed.

How to be a frugal father

Since you're going to be financing your offspring for at *least* the next sixteen years (hopefully not the next forty. . .) it pays (literally) to think ahead and take some small steps towards a more economical life. By saving here and there on everyday costs you can help put money towards your kids' education, future home or just that weekend away together that the family are in need of. Here are some suggestions to getting into that frugal mindset:

❖ **Think ahead before doing shopping.** Don't go crazy on the 3 for 2s just because they're on offer. If they're not food you or your family are keen on then don't buy. Meals with a pasta or rice base are very economical, and it's always a good idea to make more than you need so you can pop it in the freezer and have it for another meal. Minced beef or lamb is a very handy and cost-effective base for pasta or rice sauces or fillings.

❖ **Grow your own fruit and veg.** This is one that can be so much fun for the whole family because you can all get involved. Buy the kids their own seed trays or propagators and packs of seeds from the local garden centre, and help them tend the plants until they're fully grown. Make sure they all have a different type of plant to tend, so you have a good variety. You can grow lettuces, radishes, cress, all sorts of herbs . . . Tomatoes in compost bags are always very handy to grow too. Get planting today and save on your groceries!

❖ **Don't fall for emotional blackmail.** Your kids might beg you to buy the newest toy/latest fad. They might throw a tantrum, they might moan that their friends have more than them, but unless it's a one-off and they've wanted it a long time – or have done something special to deserve it – you shouldn't give in to their demands or it'll never end. Remember, that 'new thing' will be the 'old-thing-they-don't-want-to-touch-with-a-barge-pole' in a couple of weeks' time.

Playing board games with them and getting them out of doors instead of always sitting in front of the computer or TV will give them the social interaction and fresh air they need – and memories to last them a lifetime. Who's going to look back on their childhood and say 'Remember the day I got to level ten of such-and-such a game on the Playstation?'

They *will* remember playing footie with their dad, though. And in the process you'll have saved yourself a fortune in various gizmos, gadgets and electricity.

❖ **Take kids to the library to rent DVDs and books.** Sadly libraries are being utilized less and less, and without any good cause. Renting books and DVDs from the library saves pennies and supports your local community. Also, if they don't like the book you've loaned out for them they can take it back – not so easy if you've bought it and they've read their way through the book and bent the spine!

❖ **Car share on the school run.** The best thing, of course, is to walk to school together. But if this isn't an option, speak to the parents of some of your kid's friends about a car share, or get chatting at the school gates and see if you can pool resources. It'll save you all petrol and of course that exceptionally valuable commodity – time.

❖ **Reuse and recycle!** If you have more than one child, make sure any clothes in good condition are handed down (if they're the same sex of course!). It might seem that they're not getting their 'own' clothes, but often they'll be jealous of what their elder siblings are wearing, and excited to be able to give the clothes a second life.

❖ **Look after the pennies . . .** There are lots of smaller, suprising ways in which you can save money as well: instead of using the dishwasher every night, wash the dishes and let them dry naturally; don't leave the heating on overnight; take short showers; use energy-saving lightbulbs; never leave the taps running when brushing your teeth. It all adds up, and before you know it you've saved enough for that special family day out you'd been planning.

> *'I'm thinking about naming my first son Emmy so I can say I've got one. I want Emmy, Oscar and Tony – and my daughter Grammy.'*
> NOAH WYLE, US ACTOR

Dads of yesteryear

DADS ARE AN inspiration to their offspring. Every boy wants to grow up to be just like his dad and every girl uses her father as a yardstick to see whether the boys vying for her attention really cut the mustard. On the other hand, some kids have the opportunity to see exactly where dad has gone wrong in life and avoid the pitfalls that put paid to his proudest plans. History is littered with examples of dads who have either truly inspired their children or simply inspired caution, as the following stories show . . .

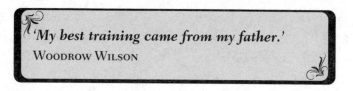

'My best training came from my father.'
WOODROW WILSON

Work experience on the high seas

It's a familiar cry: 'Can I come to work with you, Dad? Oh, please, please, pleeeeeeeese?' A certain young Marco's dad eventually gave in, saying something like, 'Okay, then, but let your mother know that you'll be late home.' In the end, they were *very* late home. They didn't come back for twenty-four years.

Marco Polo is a name that most people know and, if asked, most people would tell you that he discovered China. In fact, China was very much a discovered country long before Marco Polo visited. What Marco Polo did was to write, or cooperate with the writing of, a book about his adventures called *Il Milione* or *The Travels of Marco Polo*. The book, written around 1299, told the story of how Marco Polo travelled with his father, Niccolo, and his uncle, Maffeo, to the court of the great Mongol ruler and Emperor of China, Kublai Khan.

Marco, Niccolo and Maffeo had set out from their home in Venice as traders when Marco was around eighteen years old, but it was not the older men's first trip to the Far East. They had visited China before and as well as bringing back trade goods, they had delivered a diplomatic message from Kublai Khan to the Pope.

When young Marco reached China with his father and uncle, he soon became an important and trusted employee of the great Khan, travelling far and wide across China on official business.

Marco eventually returned home to Venice, ultimately settling down to raise his own family and enjoy the life of a highly successful merchant. But he'd never have got anywhere if his dad hadn't agreed to take him along on that business trip in 1269.

Why don't you draw me a nice picture?

The son of Messer Piero Fruosino di Antonio, a lawyer from Florence in the fifteenth century, was well known as a talented artist in the area around the hill town of Vinci where they lived. Legend has it that when a peasant asked Piero if his son might paint a small plaque to decorate his home, the proud father was happy for his son to oblige.

Young Leonardo had been born out of wedlock and had lived with his mother's family for the first five years of his life, before going to live in the house his father shared with his grandparents. His skill and intelligence quickly made a big impression on the locals but the story of the plaque didn't work out quite as you might have expected. Leonardo did paint a picture but, rather than a tranquil view of the peaceful Tuscan hills, he created a vivid, terrifying image of grotesque, fire-breathing serpents. Realizing this disturbing painting was not what quite what the peasant had in mind, Piero sold it to an art dealer who, in turn, sold it to the Duke of Milan. With the proceeds from the sale, Piero bought the peasant a more suitable artwork for his home.

Leonardo was always encouraged in his artistic endeavours, however, and at the age of fourteen he became an apprentice to the successful Florentine artist Verrocchio. Leonardo would, of course, go on to become the most famous artist, sculptor, inventor, architect, scientist and mathematician in history. He was generally known by the name of the town that had been his home – Leonardo da Vinci.

But it was his dad who recognized his talent by selling his first painting!

'A stodgy parent is no fun at all. What a child wants and deserves is a parent who is sparky.'
ROALD DAHL

Dos and don'ts for dads: supporting act

....

❖ **Do** cheer, shout encouragement and applaud good moves by any of the participants, not just your own child, unless it's your daughter's ballet class.

....

❖ **Do** wear a scarf or hat in the team colours but resist the temptation to turn up wearing the complete kit, especially if it's your daughter's ballet class.

....

❖ **Do** pay attention. It will hurt a lot if you are hit by a stray hockey ball or a flying rugby winger, but the javelin's the worst.

....

❖ **Don't** get over-excited and shout things at the ref that children, children's mothers, delicate sports coaches and sensitive referees had best not hear.

....

❖ **Don't** bring beer – it inevitably leads to *so* many other 'Don'ts'.

....

Keeping her feet on the ground

When Edwin took his two daughters, ten-year-old Millie and her little sister Grace, to the State Fair in Des Moines, Iowa, in 1907, the girls were hugely excited. There were fairground rides and stalls of all kinds at the fair, but one of the biggest attractions was a flying machine – one of the earliest types of aircraft. It was four years since the Wright brothers had made their first powered flights at Kitty Hawk in North Carolina, but now these fragile-looking, string-and-fabric, kite-like machines were beginning to appear at all sorts of public events, with intrepid pilots offering the braver members of the public short flights for a small fee.

Edwin encouraged his daughters to have a go, but Millie was not impressed with the flying machine and insisted that they went back to the merry-go-round instead. It was fourteen years later when Edwin again found himself studying an aircraft alongside his eldest daughter, this time in California.

Millie, now known by her more grown-up, proper name of Amelia, was far more impressed with the new, modern-looking biplane. Edwin paid $10 for Amelia to take a short flight, and from the moment she was airborne Amelia knew that all she wanted to do was to become an aviator.

Within four years Amelia Earhart had achieved international fame by becoming the first woman to fly the Atlantic, and in 1932 she was awarded the Distinguished Flying Cross by Congress when she crossed the Atlantic solo – all thanks to a little encouragement from good old Dad!

Girls will be girls

One of the most prolific dads in ancient history, or at least in Greek mythology, is Zeus. As King of the Gods, there was no being more powerful than Zeus, but he used his divine status in a very mortal manner, wooing lovers not only among his fellow gods, but also among the nymphs and mortals – in fact, pretty much anywhere he fancied.

Being a god, of course, he was incredibly fertile and had dozens of children but he was a bit worried when one of his wives, Metis, became pregnant, because he had been warned that she would have fearfully powerful children who might overthrow him. So he ate her.

To us, this might not seem like a practical method of birth control, but to Zeus it was very much a traditional form of family planning. His father, the Titan Cronus, had eaten all of Zeus's brothers and sisters as soon as they were born, having been told, like

Zeus, that one of his kids had it in for him. Of course, it was the child that Cronus didn't eat, Zeus, who eventually confronted his father, rescuing his brothers and sisters by slicing open Cronus's stomach.

Zeus should have known, therefore, that eating his pregnant wife would probably have serious repercussions and, sure enough, Zeus's daughter, Athena, burst out of his forehead one morning, fully grown, armed to the teeth and dressed for battle. Before he could say, 'You're not going anywhere looking like that, my girl!' she had become the Goddess of Warfare. Zeus was none the worse for the appearance of Athena, but every dad should spare him a thought before they complain about daughters being such a headache!

'My father had a profound influence on me. He was a lunatic.'
SPIKE MILLIGAN

Like father, like son

It will come as no surprise to anyone that, when he was at school, Hermann Einstein's favourite subject was mathematics. He was, after all, to become the father of one of the greatest scientific minds the world had ever known, and he certainly helped to ignite the curiosity of his son, Albert, in physical science. The gadgets helped. Dads and their boys all love playing with gadgets and Hermann was well acquainted with the latest technical hardware.

Hermann ran an electrical business with one of his brothers, Jakob, manufacturing meters and dynamos. If that wasn't enough to get his young son interested in technology, then around 1883, when four-year-old Albert was ill in bed, Hermann gave him a simple pocket compass to look at.

Young Einstein was completely fascinated by the way that, no matter which way he turned the compass, the needle always pointed in the same direction; years later he maintained that he had realized straight away that there was a force at work on the compass needle. But what was that force and how did it work? Einstein recalled that the needle in that compass pointed him towards a life of science. Well done, Dad!

Nobel lessons

Wladyslaw Sklodowski was a dad who understood the value of a good education more than most. Wladyslaw was teaching mathematics and physics in a school in Warsaw when, in 1867, the youngest of his five children was born. Like Wladyslaw's other children, the little girl, Marie, grew to love hearing her father read them stories.

What Wladyslaw read to his children were not the usual kids' stories, but works of classic literature. He often translated them into Polish as he went along. The family was not wealthy, with both Wladyslaw and his wife working as teachers, but while he may not have been able to provide financial security for his children, he certainly passed on his intellect and a wealth of knowledge.

Marie was a gifted student throughout her early years and was to become the first female professor at the prestigious Sorbonne in Paris. Having met and married French scientist Pierre Curie, Marie Sklodowska-Curie also became the first woman to receive a Nobel Prize (for Physics) and the first person ever to receive two Nobel Prizes (the second one for Chemistry). These, along with her other awards, were earned at a time when the establishment was very reluctant to recognize the achievements of women.

Sadly, Marie's mother had died when she was still only twelve and Wladyslaw passed away in 1902, the year before Marie received her first Nobel Prize, but, given all that she had achieved up to then, you can bet that he was one of the proudest Dads on the planet.

Dad's a laugh

DADS TELL BRILLIANT jokes – at least they're brilliant when kids hear them for the first time, aged four. By the time they're fourteen, the laugh's usually on Dad. Classic 'dad jokes' try hard to be funny, but are generally unintentionally so. When you have young kids it doesn't matter – things that aren't remotely funny become hilarious because they will giggle away at anything and everything.

There is a childish delight in laughter for laughter's sake that we lose as we grow older. A child can say something unintentionally hilarious, without realizing that what has been said is even remotely funny, then, when Dad starts laughing, join in because laughing is fun. What's the joke? Is there a joke? Why does it matter? Let's just laugh anyway.

Here is a collection of jokes and funny stories to groan to!

Dads' classics

The Angel Gabriel bumped into God in Heaven one day and said: 'You're looking a bit tired, God. What have you been up to?'

'Well,' said God, yawning, 'I've just invented a twenty-four-hour period for the world, part of which will be light and part of which will be darkness.'

'No wonder you're tired,' said Gabriel.

'Yes,' said God. 'I think I'll call it a day.'

—— ❖ ——

A bear walked into a clothes shop.

'Can I help you?' said the assistant.

'Yes,' said the bear. 'I'd like a fur coat, please.'

'Why would a bear want a fur coat?' asked the assistant.

'Well,' said the bear, 'I'd look pretty stupid in an anorak!'

—— ❖ ——

A man went to the doctor's and said: 'Doctor! Doctor! You've got to help me! I keep thinking I'm a smelly old Labrador.'

'I see,' said the doctor. 'Lie down on the couch, please.'

'I can't,' said the man. 'I'm not allowed on the furniture.'

—— ❖ ——

'Ouch!' yelled a man. 'A wasp just stung me on the ear!'

'Which one?' asked his wife.

'I don't know,' said the man. 'All wasps look the same to me.'

—— ❖ ——

A woman took her parrot to the vet.

'What seems to be the problem?' said the vet.

'I don't know,' said the woman, 'but poor Polly has gone right off her seed.'

'I see,' said the vet, staring into the parrot's eyes. 'Well, I think it's a simple tummy bug. Give her these tablets and she'll be better in a week. Oh, and that will be £75, please.'

'How much?' screeched the women. 'You can't charge me £75 when you've hardly even looked at her. I want a more thorough examination.'

'Very well,' said the vet. 'Nurse, bring in Goldie.'
A nurse brought in a large Labrador, who sniffed at the parrot, then barked twice before being led out again.

'Now bring in Felix,' said the vet, and the nurse returned with a black-and-white cat. The parrot cowered as the vet held the cat over her and slowly passed the cat all over the parrot, from head to tail. The cat then miaowed once and purred three times.

'Yes, it's definitely a tummy bug,' said the vet. 'Give her the tablets and she'll be better in a week. Oh, and that will be £250, please.'

'What?' cried the woman. 'Why has the price gone up so much?'

'Well,' explained the vet, 'now you've had the Lab tests and the cat scan.'

> 'She got her looks from her father.
> He's a plastic surgeon.'
> GROUCHO MARX

Changing times

Neil had always been known for taking pride in his appearance. He bucked the modern trends in that he liked to have polished shoes (he even cleaned his trainers), pressed trousers and ironed shirts. His shirt collection was, in fact, something of which he was particularly proud. He always had a clean-shaven look and there was never a hair out of place on his head. His fussiness was a standing joke amongst his friends, who often referred to him as 'Neat Neil'.

None of this changed when he married Alison. He continued to iron his own shirts – and anything that Alison needed to be ironed into the bargain. He was overjoyed when Alison became pregnant, although some of his friends felt that he seemed more worried than most at the prospect of becoming a dad.

When the new baby arrived, Neil and Alison invited some friends round on a Sunday afternoon to meet baby Kyle. The visitors made all the right noises about the beautiful baby boy, but all were struck by Neil's appearance. Everyone expects new parents to look slightly sleep deprived, but compared with the 'old', pre-baby Neat Neil, this Neil looked positively dishevelled. His hair had a slightly wild look and he had a stubbly beard – but he beamed with pride when he and Alison showed off their son.

Alison handed Kyle to Neil while she went to make some tea and Neil held his son close, Kyle's head resting on his Dad's shoulder. It was as Neil paced back and forth, chatting about the baby, that his friends all spotted 'it'.

'Neil,' said one of them gently, 'the baby seems to have thrown up down the back of your shirt.'

'Oh,' said Neil, 'don't worry about that – it's been there since yesterday . . .'

Changed times, indeed!

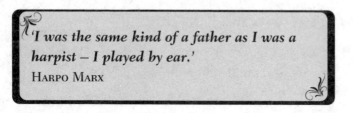

'I was the same kind of a father as I was a harpist – I played by ear.'
HARPO MARX

Silly things dads say

❖ 'Put the cat out? I didn't even know it was on fire.'

❖ 'You're thirsty? How do you do, I'm Friday.'

❖ 'If you break your legs, don't come running to me.'

❖ 'You will lie still and go to sleep – and I don't care if it takes all night.'

❖ 'Keep your mouth closed when you're eating.'

True silly things kids said

❖ 'My dad goes to the gym twice a week so he can drink beer.'

❖ 'Oysters' balls are called pearls.'

❖ 'If the sea goes all round, you are an island. If it doesn't, you are incontinent.'

❖ 'I'm not out of breath. There's plenty more inside.'

Double trouble

When Ian and Melanie discovered that Melanie was expecting twins, they were both overjoyed, but the thought that twins would mean twice as much work for the new parents was more than a little worrying. Ian took advice and read everything he could about twins, eventually coming to the conclusion that having twins was actually quite a good thing – having children of the same age means that each has a natural companion and playmate, for a start. Melanie was less convinced, but Ian promised that he would pull his weight when it came to bringing up the twins.

He was as good as his word when the two baby girls were born, changing nappies, preparing meals (not just for his daughters) and sharing the chores as best he could.

The twins became more of a handful after a few months once they started to move around more. Left alone with the girls while Melanie was out one afternoon, Ian laid them both down on changing mats on the living room floor – he and Melanie had long since learned that the twins were calmer, keeping each other company, if dealt with in this way.

No sooner had he unfastened one of the girls' nappies than he realized that he was going to need more 'wipes' and dashed off to fetch some from the bathroom. When he returned a moment later, he was horrified to find the girls 'helping' with the housework.

Both had managed to remove their nappies completely and had crawled over to a sideboard unit where they were smearing the contents of their nappies all over the drawer fronts, 'polishing' the furniture just like they has seen Mum and Dad do!

Ian had a great deal of clearing up to do before Melanie got home.

Dads will be boys

ONE OF THE most loveable things about Dad is that, at heart, he's still just a kid. He might play the serious adult when the situation calls for it, but give him half a chance and he'll be playing the same tricks his ten-year-old self used to get up to. The following true stories show just how little Dad ever really grows up.

The daredevil

Hilary's dad was celebrating his ninetieth birthday and she dutifully arranged to go to see him on the big day. Even though the drive to Dad's house took over three hours, Hilary, her husband and her young daughter made the trip on a regular basis and spoke to Dad on the phone or emailed the internet-savvy 'silver surfer' almost every day, especially since Hilary's mother had died a few years previously. She considered that they were a close family, despite how far apart they lived, so she was very concerned when they arrived at Dad's house, singing 'Happy Birthday' on the doorstep, to be greeted by her father wearing a grave face.

'Come in, I've got something I want to show you,' was all that Dad said.

They followed him into his living room where he asked them to sit down. By this point Hilary was expecting some truly dreadful news and her mind was racing through all of the possibilities. A dreadful illness? A financial crisis? Some horrific secret from Dad's unknown criminal past? She had no idea what to expect.

Her father picked up a DVD case and removed the disc, slipping it into the player. There was a gush of rushing wind noise as the sound made it to the speakers before the picture hit the screen and all three visitors stared in amazement as Dad appeared on the TV plummeting through the air in a skydive! Nervously avoiding eye contact, he explained that it was something that he had always wanted to do, so he had decided to treat himself for his big birthday and booked himself a tandem skydive, jumping from the aircraft strapped into a harness with an instructor. He'd had to do some training for the jump, the skydiving team made sure that he was fit enough for it and his doctor had confirmed that there was no medical impediment to prevent him doing the jump. Hilary was almost speechless.

'But we would have loved to come to see you do your jump,' she said. 'Why didn't you tell us you were doing this?'

'Well . . .' said Dad, 'I didn't think you'd let me . . .'

'The one thing I remember about Christmas was that my father used to take me out in a boat about ten miles offshore on Christmas Day, and I used to have to swim back. Extraordinary. It was a ritual. Mind you, that wasn't the hard part. The difficult bit was getting out of the sack.'
JOHN CLEESE

Madman on the loose

Children who have been stuck indoors for too long can easily start to go a bit 'stir crazy' with the familiar 'I'm so-o-o-o-o-o bored' refrain usually preceding a period of boisterous mayhem. Finding himself on the end of his children's wailing complaints one day, British politician Tony Benn decided to liven things up a bit for them.

He answered a telephone call in their London home, announcing that the police had just informed him that a dangerous criminal maniac was on the loose in their neighbourhood. He warned the kids that they should check the doors were locked and that all of the windows were firmly secured. The children rushed around the house, peering out into the street to see if they could spot the mad murderer lurking in the shadows as they double-checked the windows.

Then they heard a noise coming from the top of the house. It sounded like someone blundering around on the roof! The children all froze, their eyes wide with terror . . . until they heard their dad chuckling merrily. He had hoodwinked them all with a perfectly planned prank. The former Minister of Technology then revealed how he had made the telephone ring and how he had rigged a device to make a thumping noise up on the roof.

They would think twice before complaining about being bored again!

Dos and don'ts for dads: fun in the snow

- ❖ **Do** join in when a snowball fight erupts in the park, in the garden or even right outside your house when you've just come home from work.

- ❖ **Do** fall backwards in the snow to make a snow 'angel', even if you are wearing your best suit (those with bad backs are excused, though).

- ❖ **Do** help your kids and their friends to build the biggest snowman ever.

- ❖ **Do** organize a squad to flatten a 'Cresta Run' on the slope in the park for faster sledging and 'ringo' rides.

- ❖ **Don't** go showing off by turning up at the park with your old skis or trying to do the Cresta Run standing up on a sledge or a ringo. The kids won't take time off from having fun in the snow to come and visit you in hospital.

- ❖ **Don't** ever be tempted to show the kids how to write their name in the snow!

85

Snow joke

When the snow started falling thick and fast one wintry Sunday, Steve decided to take his son, Josh, and daughter, Ashley, out for some fun in the white stuff. Steve knew just the place to go sledging: there was a slope in a field on the outskirts of town that he and his friends had used when they were kids. So he dug his old wooden sledge out of the attic, rubbed down the metal runners with some sandpaper to shine them up and loaded it into his car along with the kids and their inflatable 'ringo'.

The snow was lying deep enough for sledging but the roads had all been gritted and were clear enough for the short drive. Steve parked near the field and they all piled out of the car, hurling snowballs at each other as they made their way to the top of the slope. There was no one else around so they had the whole field to themselves.

The rubber ringo was great for flattening out a smooth run, packing down the snow and making it easier for the old sledge to get up to top speed. Josh and Ashley built a little ramp halfway down the slope to form a jump for their ringo. Steve took photographs of them with his phone, then decided that he would try out the jump, as well. Despite his kids warning him that he should do it in the bouncy, inflatable ringo, which provided its own soft landing pad, he was determined to do it on his old sledge. He hit the ramp and took off, parting company with the sledge in mid-air. He somersaulted, hitting the slope on his bottom and feeling a jarring pain in his back that immediately became a hundred times worse when the sledge slammed into him.

Josh and Ashley, at first in fits of laughter, quickly realized that all was not well and rushed down the slope to help their Dad. Steve didn't think that he could move. He told the kids that they would have to call for an ambulance, but when Josh fished the phone out of his father's pocket, it was smashed to pieces.

There was nothing else for it. Josh and Ashley helped Steve into the ringo then dragged and pushed him back to the car. They then manhandled him into the driving seat, from where he was able gingerly to guide the car to the hospital. The bruising and the torn ligament were easier to bear than the lambasting he received when his wife arrived to take them all home . . .

'My Dad used to say "always fight fire with fire", which is probably why he got thrown out of the fire brigade.'
PETER KAY

The old ones are the best

Alan had a couple of days off work during the school summer holidays as part of the rota he and his wife had worked out, along with some friends, to make sure that there was always proper childcare for the kids. His eleven-year-old son, William, had had a sleepover with a friend who lived just a few houses away and the two boys were due to deliver themselves to Alan's house around ten in the morning. Alan was up early preparing a surprise for the boys.

He rooted out all the Scalextric slot car racing track that he and William had accumulated over the years and set about building a massive racing circuit outside on the patio. Alan had decided a bit of fresh air would do the boys good, because he knew they would otherwise spend all of their time together playing computer games. He took over two hours to piece together the circuit he had planned, finishing just as the boys arrived.

The two eleven-year-olds bumbled through the house carrying their PSP electronic games consoles. Alan led them out to the patio, revealing his racing circuit with a flourish. Both boys looked distinctly underwhelmed. As he disappeared indoors to make the boys a snack, Alan heard William sigh and whisper to his friend, 'Dad loves this stuff. We'd better play with it for a little while, or he'll only get upset.'

But Alan's efforts had not been in vain. Three hours later the boys were still racing, completely won over by the magic of miniature motor sport!

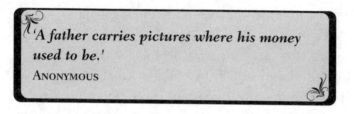

'A father carries pictures where his money used to be.'
ANONYMOUS

Clowning around

When Martin's daughter, Clare, was seven years old, Martin and his wife, Chris, decided to have a birthday party for her. Most of Clare's friends had been having parties at special venues like bowling alleys, theme parks or leisure centres where catering was laid on and the entertainment provided for the children made the party an unforgettable event. All of that, of course, comes at a price and Martin and Chris were a bit short of cash. They didn't want Clare to miss out on having a birthday party, so they decided to have the party at home, the old-fashioned way.

Chris worked hard to prepare lots of party food, including a huge birthday cake, and Martin's job was to keep them all entertained. He organized games of pass-the-parcel, musical statues and musical chairs, which led to much screaming and excitement amongst the two dozen children squeezed into the living room.

To settle them all down while they were being fed, Martin decided to become what every child loves – a clown. At least, he thought every child loves clowns. Martin disappeared while Chris and a couple of other helpful mums settled the children on the living room floor with their food on paper plates, then re-appeared wearing an old t-shirt and with his face made-up in white and red like a reject from a *Batman* movie. Some of the children looked stunned, others just looked terrified.

Needless to say, Martin had complete silence as he stood in front of the table on which stood the untouched birthday cake, running through a series of 'knock-knock' jokes, enjoying neither a word of response nor even a titter of appreciation from his stunned audience. It was not going well and the party atmosphere had all but evaporated. Realizing that he was getting nowhere, Martin grabbed some balloons, as he had previously practised blowing them up to make balloon animals.

The first sausage-shaped balloon inflated easily along its entire length, then exploded in Martin's face. He stumbled backwards, lost his footing and fell onto the table, destroying the birthday cake and managing to pull down the curtains from the nearby window into the bargain. After a short pause, the whole room erupted into squeals of laughter.

None of the party guests ever forgot Clare's dad the clown or the best birthday party ever!

My dad can do that!

THERE ARE CERTAIN things that every child would like to be able to boast that their dad can do – like driving a Formula 1 car, flying a space shuttle or splitting concrete blocks with his forehead. The sensible dad avoids as many of these things as possible, including walking over red hot coals, eating light bulbs, wrestling alligators and towing a ten-ton truck using a cable attached to his nipples.

There are some things that will impress your child, however, which you can learn quite easily without ending up having to undertake extensive training with NASA, knitting asbestos socks or tucking your nipples into your pants.

Here are a few things that dads and kids can do together . . .

'When I look at the smiles on all the children's faces, I just know they're about to jab me with something.'
HOMER SIMPSON

Make giant bubbles

On a summer's day there is nothing more fun for kids of all ages than making gigantic bubbles. Get everyone out in the garden or park, and make sure you're all involved. Creating the bubble-making solution and the bubble-blowing wand is all part of the fun. Follow the instructions overleaf and you're guaranteed to have a day that is full of giggling kids and magical bubbles.

'It was my father who taught me to value myself. He told me that I was uncommonly beautiful and that I was the most precious thing in his life.'
DAWN FRENCH

WHAT YOU'LL NEED:
    1 cup washing up liquid
    4 cups water
    $\frac{1}{4}$ cup glycerin
    a washing-up bowl or plastic storage box
    a ball of string
    6-inch bendy straws

1. To create the wand with which you make the bubbles, cut some string about 24 inches long and insert the string through two plastic bendy straws. Pull the string tight so the straws are shaped into a square or rectangle, then tie a knot in the string and insert the knot inside one of the straws.

2. Take your plastic bowl or washing up bowl and pour in one part washing-up liquid to four parts water (one cup to four should work) then add a quarter of a cup of glycerin, which helps strengthen the walls of the bubbles so they don't pop so quickly.

3. Dip the 'wand' into the solution, taking care to pull it taut, then gently raise it out again. You should have a thin filmy layer in the middle of the straws – if you don't, dip it again.

4. Carefully lift the wand, taking care to stand with the wind behind you, and if there's a light wind it should push a bubble out with it. However, if it's a still day, simply walk backwards slowly and the air will press against the filmy layer to create a bubble.

5. If the bubble is reluctant to come out completely, try closing the straws together to push it out.

6. Sometimes you can get more than one bubble out of one dip, but if not simply return the wand to the solution and get making more bubbles! It's so simple but a great deal of fun.

Create a sand city

You've been on the beach for a couple of hours, the kids are tired of playing with the beach ball and the jellyfish are putting everyone off swimming. It's time for Dad to get his thinking cap on. And quite frankly, a tired old sandcastle just won't cut it. Yes, this situation calls for some serious creativity – and the desire to get your hands covered in sand.

Assuming not every dad is going to be Michelangelo when it comes to sand sculpting, the trick is to go to the beach prepared – with jelly moulds. These days you can get all sorts of shapes, including buildings, animals and cars. So either raid the kitchen and see what moulds you have in the pantry, or buy some in the store or online beforehand.

Then all you need to do when the kids start to get restless is take out the moulds and get everyone filling them with sand to create a miniature sand city. Encourage them to add bits on to the mould-shaped sand figures once they've set and, if they're creative, to try and build their own without the shapes to help them. This should keep them busy until home time!

My dad can't do that

Helping with homework is a chore that most dads dread. Like everything else to do with your kids, if you are to share properly in their development, supervising homework is something in which both partners have to take a hand. Just like their kids, however, parents have different skills, strengths and weaknesses. John and Kate agreed from the very first day that their eldest child, Michael, went to school, that Kate would be the best one to help with Michael's reading, writing and spelling, while John would have to deal with the maths.

John took this responsibility very seriously. The modern methods used for teaching maths were vastly different to the way he had been taught at primary school, so by the time Michael was nine years old, Dad was working hard to keep up. He went through all of the exercises in Michael's maths books, learning new ways to approach not only adding, subtracting, multiplying and dividing, but also the new ways in which children were being encouraged to explore the relationships between numbers.

It meant a good deal of reading and a lot of practising tricky sums, usually after a long, hard day at work, but John reckoned he was keeping one step ahead of Michael to help guide his son through any areas in which he was having difficulty. Then came Michael's first big maths test, and John was the proudest dad in the school when Michael passed with the top marks in his class. John asked Michael's teacher for a blank test paper so that, just for fun, he could sit the test, too. To his horror, and Michael's delight, John failed.

Naturally, John was never allowed to forget this, but Michael still asked for his Dad's help when he had a problem with his maths.

Carve a pumpkin lantern

Halloween just wouldn't be the same without pumpkin lanterns. For most people, it's the only time of year that they ever even see a pumpkin. They may be a seasonal crop, but so are apples and we seem to be able to get them all year round. Perhaps, then, pumpkins wouldn't be the same without Halloween. That's when people think about buying them and most pumpkins are bought not to be eaten but to be carved into lanterns. So dads really need to know how to do it, don't they?

All you need is a sharp kitchen knife and a marker pen, but for intricate work you can buy special little pumpkin carving tools and paper templates featuring some very fancy designs.

1. The first thing to do is give your pumpkin a wipe with a damp cloth, and as pumpkin carving can be a messy business, lay some newspaper down on the table to work on. The first step in the carving process is to lop the top off the pumpkin, but you have to be careful. Using a sharp kitchen knife, cut a hole in the top of the pumpkin, with the stalk, or the bit where the stalk used to be, in the centre of the section you are about to remove. You don't need to make the hole too big, but it will have to be big enough for you to be able to get your hand inside to scoop out the seeds and some of the flesh. Push the knife into the pumpkin at an angle running in towards the core, moving it all the way round so that the section you remove is narrower at its base on the inside than at its top on the outside. This ensures that when you replace this piece as a 'lid' to your lantern, it doesn't fall straight through.

2. Once you have removed your lid, which will involve pushing the knife in to cut away some of the straggly stuff inside, scoop out the seeds and some of the flesh. Have a pot or some kind of

container standing by in which to dump the insides. A metal spoon works well for scooping out, but you may have to remove stubborn areas by scraping with a knife. Don't be tempted to remove too much flesh from the 'walls' of your lantern. An expert carver can create all sorts of glowing effects through thin layers of skin on the walls, but thicker walls are more robust for less experienced carvers and help the lantern to last longer. All you really have to do is make it neat and clean inside.

3. Now you are ready to decide on your design. You can draw a face directly onto the pumpkin and carefully cut out some eyes and a jagged mouth by pushing your knife through the wall of the pumpkin. Another option is to draw a design on a piece of thin paper. This gives you a better chance to experiment and to agree on the look of the thing with the child who will undoubtedly be hovering at your shoulder ready to 'help'. You can then tape the paper to the part of the pumpkin that you want to use as the face (some pumpkins have a flat area that lends itself well to this) and, using a small nail or a drawing pin, push holes through the paper into the pumpkin along the lines of your design. When you pull the paper away you will be left with a pumpkin with the design traced onto it in little holes.

4. If you have 'traced' a design onto your pumpkin, you now need to start cutting. Push the knife or carving tool all the way through the wall and cut along the lines of the design. Don't try to remove an entire design element in one piece. Cutting all the way round the mouth, for instance, will seldom work, and you may lose one of the 'teeth' you spent so much time drawing and cutting around. Instead, cut out chunks of the mouth, which will help to preserve your design as you progress.

5. Once you have finished carving, pop a candle inside on the 'floor' of your lantern. The best (and safest) thing to use is a tea light that comes in its own little metal cup.

Now all you have to do is to light your lantern and turn out the lights for the full terrifying effect!

> *'To be a successful father, there's one absolute rule: when you have a kid, don't look at it for the first two years.'*
> ERNEST HEMINGWAY

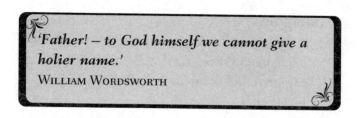

'Father! – to God himself we cannot give a holier name.'
WILLIAM WORDSWORTH

Make a pizza

Every child would love to be able to walk into the local pizza place, point to the chef spinning wobbly great discs of pizza dough in mid air and say, 'My Dad can do that.' Well you're not going to learn that here. Making pizza dough is a messy business, especially if, as you should do, you involve the kids in the process. Once you start flinging the stuff around the kitchen you will quickly find yourself standing in what looks like the aftermath of a bun fight in a bakery, wearing a pizza base as a hat.

However, it's straightforward enough to make yourself a pizza if, rather than going through the fiddly business of making your own pizza base – which isn't really too complicated but is time consuming – just buy a few. You can find plain pizza bases in most supermarkets. While you are there, you might like to pick up a jar of pizza tomato sauce. Again, it makes the whole process a bit easier.

Otherwise, you will need:

INGREDIENTS:

1 jar passata Italian tomato sauce (unless you are
    using pizza sauce)

1 teaspoonful of dried basil (unless it is in the
    pizza sauce)

1 crushed garlic clove (unless there is garlic in the
    pizza sauce)

125g ball of mozzarella cheese, sliced

Grated parmesan cheese

10 cherry tomatoes, cut in half

6 mushrooms, thinly sliced

Some sliced sausage or slices of ham torn into
    pieces roughly the same size as the
    mushrooms

1 tablespoon of olive oil

WHAT YOU HAVE TO DO:

1.   Pre-heat your oven to 220°C, Gas Mark 7.

2.   If you are using the passata, mix it with the basil
     and garlic.

3.   Spread the passata or pizza sauce generously over
     the pizza base. The best way to do this is to use a
     spoon to drop a dollop onto the base, then use the
     back of the spoon to spread the dollop out over a
     small area. Keep adding sauce until you have
     covered the whole thing – not *too* much, mind!

4. Cover the sauce with the mozzarella slices. This isn't like tiling a bathroom floor; you can leave some gaps. Just make sure that when the cheese melts it will spread out over the whole pizza.

5. Arrange your cherry tomato halves over the pizza, spreading them out so that when the pizza is sliced, they will be evenly distributed.

6. Arrange your mushrooms and sausage or ham in the same manner as the cherry tomato halves.

7. Drizzle a little olive oil lightly over the whole lot, then scatter a dusting of parmesan cheese on top.

8. Place the pizza on a greased baking tray and bake it in the oven for ten minutes or until it goes golden brown on top.

If your kids don't like mushrooms, experiment with your own toppings – sliced peppers or chunks of pineapple, for example, or tuna flakes instead of ham. The great thing is that making a pizza is a fun thing for dads to do with kids. It's also relatively quick, so it doesn't tax the kids' attention span or Dad's patience too much!

Bon appetit!

Dad knows best

The architect Daedalus was a very clever man, not only a highly talented draughtsman who was said to be able to make moving images, but also extremely skilled in the use of all sorts of tools. Daedalus designed the Labyrinth at Knossos on the island of Crete. King Minos, the ruler of Crete, was blighted by the existence of a half-man, half-bull, crazed creature called the Minotaur, said to be the crossbreed offspring of Minos' wife and a bull. He commissioned Daedalus to design and build the Labyrinth as a prison maze from which the Minotaur, which was utterly ferocious but not very bright, could never escape.

Daedalus completed the Labyrinth with the help of his son, Icarus. So complex was the maze that Daedalus could hardly find his way out of it himself. In order that the design and construction of the Labyrinth should remain a secret, however, King Minos decided to keep Daedalus and Icarus as his prisoners on the island.

Locked in a high tower for much of the time, Daedalus and Icarus had no opportunity to escape. The only way off the island was by boat and news would reach King Minos in an instant if either of them attempted to board a ship. But then Daedalus came up with a cunning plan. He watched sea birds drifting past their prison tower and decided that they should fly away from the island just like birds.

Daedalus studied the birds' wings, then gathered together feathers of all sizes. He fastened the feathers together using the lightest thread to secure the larger ones and a drop of wax for the smaller ones. When he had finished one set of wings, he strapped them to his arms and, waving them gently, found to his delight that his feet left the floor.

He quickly made a second set of wings and the two fledgling aviators worked out how to fly. Before they made their attempt at escape, however, Daedalus warned Icarus not to fly too low or the salt water from the sea would dissolve the delicate thread in his wings. Neither should he fly too high because the heat from the sun would melt the wax. Did the boy listen? Not a chance.

Once they had left Crete behind and flown past Samos, Delos and Lebythnos, Icarus started showing off, soaring upwards, only to find the wax on his wings melted, sending him plummeting to his death in the sea below. In memory of his son, Daedalus named the place near where Icarus fell 'Icaria'.

Top ten movie dads

The film father	The flick	The kids
1. Darth Vader	*Star Wars IV–VI*	Luke Skywalker, Princess Leia Organa
2. Mr Incredible (Bob Parr)	*The Incredibles*	Dash, Violet, Jack-Jack
3. Henry Jones Snr	*Indiana Jones and the Last Crusade*	Henry 'Indiana' Jones Jnr
4. Jack Byrnes	*Meet the Parents*	Pam, Debbie, Denny
5. Daniel Hillard	*Mrs Doubtfire*	Lydia, Chris, Natalie
6. Peter Mitchell Michael Kellam Jack Holden	*Three Men and a Baby*	Mary
7. Guido Orefice	*Life is Beautiful*	Joshua

8. Marlin	*Finding Nemo*	Nemo
9. George Banks	*Father of the Bride*	Annie, Matty, Megan
10. Arthur Weasley	The *Harry Potter* films	Bill, Charlie, Percy, Fred, George, Ron, Ginny

Build a snowman

There's no better fun to be had when the weather turns wintry white than piling outdoors to build a snowman. Apart from all the fun the kids will have, it'll make you feel as young as them!

First things first, of course you have to start matters off with a snowball fight – purely to practice making balls of snow, obviously. Then, it's a fantastically simple process, and best enjoyed with lots of hands on deck . . .

1. The basic snowman is made of two big snowballs, with the bottom one that makes up the body being the larger of the two. You can, of course, make your snowman out of three snowballs, creating a bottom and top half to his body out of two balls

and then a smaller ball on top as the head, but let's keep it simple for now. To make the body, crush a couple of handfuls of snow together, creating a snowball, then roll it along the ground so it picks up layers of snow as it is rolled.

2. Keep rolling the ball to make it larger, but not in a straight line or you will end up with a cylinder rather than a spherical shape. If it gets really big you can all pile behind it to push together!

3. When you've rolled the snowball to the size you want it, leave it where you want the snowman to be placed and repeat steps 1 and 2, but make sure that this ball is smaller – it's supposed to be the head, so has to be smaller to be in proportion, and also so that you can lift it onto the body without breaking your back.

4. Once you've done the head and popped it on top of the body, you can start decorating the snowman, and giving him proper features. The traditional ones are a carrot for his nose, coal for his eyes and mouth and twigs for his arms. Beyond that you can get creative – either sculpting the snow itself if you don't mind getting freezing cold hands, or by adding on clothes, leaves, or anything you can find.

Driving lessons

Monday night was Ken's turn to play chauffeur to his daughter, Rebecca, and her friends, picking them up from Girl Guides. He always tried to talk to his passengers on the way home, but did feel a bit awkward with these young ladies, who chatted so freely and fast amongst each other that he had difficulty keeping up.

To brighten up the journey, one evening Ken decided to teach the girls how to change gear. He showed them how the gear stick worked so that, when he called 'First gear', his helper could slip it into first, 'Second gear' she could pull the stick back into second, and so forth, with Ken operating the clutch at the right moment.

The first of Rebecca's friends caught on very quickly and thoroughly enjoyed this game. Ken could see his daughter's face in his rear view mirror and she looked happy that her friend was having fun. Ken thought he'd pulled a masterstroke, that he would now be seen as the coolest Dad in the neighbourhood. He was especially pleased with himself because he knew that impressing her friends would definitely also impress Rebecca.

When the first girl was dropped off, the second friend took the front seat and Ken encouraged her to try changing gear.

'No thanks,' said the girl.

'Don't be shy,' said Ken. 'Give it a go, then you can try the same thing with your dad.'

'I don't think so,' the girl replied. 'My dad could never let me do that.'

'Of course he could,' said Ken, heartily.

'No he couldn't,' said the girl. 'We don't have an old-fashioned gear change on our car, we have a modern automatic.'

There followed a brief silence before Ken, avoiding eye contact in the rear view mirror, switched on the radio.

Dad to the rescue

EVERY DAD'S A hero to his kids, and when the chips are down, fathers can really show that they've got what it takes to rival Clark Kent. Here are some incredible real-life stories of paternal bravery and nobility . . .

> *'I cannot think of any need in childhood as strong as the need for a father's protection.'*
> SIGMUND FREUD

Smoky mountain bear

In August 2009, Evan Pala was out on a long hike with his brother, Alex, and his dad, John, in the Great Smoky Mountains National Park in Tennessee. They were taking a breather near a stream when Evan suddenly realized that a black bear was lurking close by, staring right at him.

The black bear can be found in the wilderness all over America from Alaska to the Southern States. Although normally quite timid creatures, they are nevertheless extremely dangerous at close quarters. A male black bear can be up to seven feet (2.12 metres) tall when standing erect on its hind legs and weigh in at 660lb (300kg).

The bear stood and lunged at the eight-year-old who had time to yell 'Bear!' before the animal clamped its jaws around his arm. Evan's dad was there in an instant. He pounded the bear with his fists, pried its jaws apart to release Evan's arm then threw rocks at it until it ran off.

Evan was fortunate to escape with relatively minor injuries to his upper arm, but had it not been for his heroic dad, he might not have been so lucky.

The American dream

Umberto Baron was a young boy in Italy during the Second World War. He was fascinated by the American soldiers who set up camp near his home, especially the ones working on the trucks and jeeps in the motor pool, and he became a regular spectator. One of the GIs encouraged him to learn how to repair and maintain the vehicles. He gave Umberto American candy, showing him how the engines worked and the things a mechanic needed to know to keep a vehicle running.

Umberto never forgot the lessons his American 'buddy' taught him. He grew up to be a mechanic, moved to America and eventually ran his own successful garage business, living what is traditionally referred to as 'The American Dream'. He was flicking through a newspaper one day when, to his surprise, he saw a photograph of his old buddy from the motor pool in Italy – William Jefferson Blythe. Blythe's photograph had appeared because the media were tracking down stories about the man. He had died many years before in a car accident in 1946, leaving his young wife heavily pregnant with their first child.

That child grew up to be the President of the United States, Bill Clinton. The President knew very little about his dad's background and Umberto was able to fill him in on what an inspiration Blythe had been. President Clinton wrote in his autobiography, 'My father left me with the feeling that I had to live for two people, and that if I did it well enough, somehow I could make up for the life he should have had.'

> *'I'm a father; that's what matters most.*
> *Nothing matters more.'*
> GORDON BROWN

That's no pussy cat!

Four-year-old Paul Krismer had the shock of his young life while with his parents at the Schoen Lake Provincial Park in Nimpkish Valley on Vancouver Island. The park, famous for its dramatic scenery, is a popular destination for campers and hikers who want to get close to nature.

Paul got a good deal closer than anyone would have liked when he was attacked by a cougar. Paul's dad, also called Paul, had no idea that such a dangerous animal was close by until he heard a rustle in the undergrowth and the big cat leapt out on Paul Junior. The mountain lion's favourite method of attack is to seize its prey by the neck, but little Paul ducked when he heard something coming and the cougar's jaws clamped around his head.

Paul Senior didn't hesitate for a second, leaping on the cougar and hitting it with such force that it immediately released his son. He then stomped on the big cat as hard as he could and gave it another kick as it turned to flee. Little Paul suffered some nasty cuts and bruises but the quick reactions of his father undoubtedly saved his life.

James 'Mokie' Bond

No hero in the world, either real or fictional, has a name more easily recognizable than James Bond. Bond is adored by millions of boys and their dads. He is an entirely fictional character, yet he was based on a number of personalities who were very real.

One of them was a man known to his four boys as 'Mokie'. The strange pet name came from a small child's attempt to pronounce the word 'smokey', as Mokie was seldom seen relaxing without his trusty pipe.

Mokie was a highly intelligent man, a lawyer and a British MP, representing Henley in Parliament from 1910 until he went off to serve as an officer with the Queen's Own Oxfordshire Hussars during the First World War. He wrote to his sons regularly and was a much-respected officer. When he was killed in 1917, Winston Churchill wrote an obituary in *The Times*.

That obituary, signed by Churchill, was always kept in a frame on the wall somewhere in the home of Mokie's second son, Ian Fleming. James Bond's creator undoubtedly instilled his most famous creation with some of the heroic qualities of his gallant father, Valentine 'Mokie' Fleming, the man who inspired his four boys to end their prayers each night with '. . . and please help me to grow up to be like Mokie.'

Old pals

George Clooney and his dad, Nick, have been working together in the public eye since George was a boy. Nick Clooney was a journalist and broadcaster, working as 'anchorman' on various TV news programmes before becoming a game show host with his own show, *The Money Maze*.

George used to help out whenever his services were required, which often meant dressing up in bizarre costumes and making a fool of himself. Nick Clooney most certainly impressed his son with his skill in front of an audience and in front of a camera. George, of course, would later show his Dad that he could perform pretty well in front of the camera himself, although Nick didn't have to play dress up either in *ER* on TV or in any of George's movies.

Clooney Senior is, however, still involved in journalism. Nick and George travelled together to Darfur in Sudan in 2006 to make a documentary called *A Journey to Darfur*. The purpose of the documentary was to highlight the suffering of the people there, caught up in a secret war and violent ethnic cleansing programme. George has often said that he has no qualms about using the celebrity status he has achieved to help him campaign about things that he feels are important. He also admits to being hugely impressed by his dad's approach to such matters.

'He's brighter than I am,' said George, 'and he's the guy who, on every issue, stands up and points. He's a big old liberal. He writes for the newspaper and he just goes for everybody. God, I wish I had the nerve to do what he does.'

'My Dad always used to tell me that if they challenge you to an after-school fight, tell them you won't wait – you'll kick their ass right now.'
CAMERON DIAZ

But *how*, Dad?

KIDS ASK THE strangest questions sometimes, and dads are expected to come up with all the right answers, every time. Even the smartest father in the world isn't going to be able to maintain a hundred per cent record, however, so dads have to be able to think on their feet.

You never know what sort of question is going to be sprung on you next, but there are some that crop up on a regular basis, allowing you to spend the odd moment preparing for them in advance. To keep your mind nimble and give you a few tips on how to tackle tricky topics, take a look at the questions in this chapter. All of them have actually been asked by kids and hopefully the answers here will inspire dads everywhere to be creative when coming up with a response!

Question: *How does Santa get back up the chimney?*

Answer: You asked for it. Having spent all that time persuading your child that Santa slides down the chimney on Christmas Eve to deliver the presents, you now have to explain how a fat old man carrying a sack that presumably still contains gifts for everyone else in your street manages to climb all the way back up the chimney to the roof where he has parked his sleigh.

The best approach is to keep it logical. Children become very suspicious when they are unexpectedly required to slip their imagination into top gear. Leaping a sudden logic gap will leave them wondering if everything they have heard is complete codswallop. As far as Santa's departure is concerned, you have to build on what has previously been taken to be true. If you have a chimney, Santa can slide down it to deliver the Christmas presents. If you don't have a chimney, then Santa has to use magic fairy dust to transform himself into a sparkling shimmer that can waft through keyholes or under doors. That is also what he does when he comes down the chimney, because a big fellow like him would get stuck otherwise, wouldn't he? And he uses the magic fairy dust to help him soar back up the chimney, too.

Question: *Why are girls' bits different from boys' bits?*

Answer: Ask your mother, she knows.

Question: *How come Mummy's a good dancer and you're rubbish?*

Answer: The first thing to point out is that it's not your fault that you can't dance as well as your child's mother. So whose fault is it? Blame it on God. He did a great job creating the first man, Adam, out of dust and blowing life into him through his nostrils. But making the first man was a really complicated thing to do, so God decided to take a shortcut when it came to making the first woman, Eve.

While Adam was sleeping, God borrowed one of his ribs and made Eve out of that, so that Adam would have the nice surprise of someone to talk to when he woke up. Adam was very pleased, grateful to have some company at last, but in borrowing his rib, God had left him a bit unbalanced. Eve, being brand new, was beautifully balanced and perfectly graceful but, until the rib grew back, Adam found moving around a little more awkward than usual. To this day, some men still find it a problem.

'My parents treated me like I had a brain – which, in turn, caused me to have one.'
US ACTRESS DIANE LANE

Question: *How much does money cost?*

Answer: Don't be tempted to point to a few grey hairs on your head and say, 'See these? That's what money costs me.' You will only wake up one morning to find that you have been scalped and that your child is down at the sweet shop attempting to trade your crowning glory for a handful of jelly babies.

It takes kids a long time before they can appreciate the value of money. Once they realize that money is what you have to hand over to persuade the shopkeeper to give you what you want, children know that they need money – but how much? They have to progress a little further before they understand that if someone were to try to charge them £100 for a bar of chocolate it would not be worth it. So, like every other tricky question that children ask, there's no easy answer to this one. 'A lot' should suffice for a while.

Question: *Could a guinea pig survive in a toilet?*

Answer: The short answer, of course, is no. Guinea pigs can swim, like most other animals, but they wouldn't be first choice for the water polo team or the synchronized swimming squad at the animal Olympics. You might also explain that a guinea pig wouldn't be able to grip the ceramic surface with its claws, so, eventually, it would become tired and, unable to climb out, it would drown. A more appropriate response might be, 'Why? What have you done with your guinea pig?'

Dos and don'ts for dads: helping with homework

....

❖ **Do** try to take an interest in what your child has been given to do for homework. If you don't seem to care, then your child won't either. Not taking an interest also makes it easier for your child to keep the homework book hidden until it's time to feed it to the dog.

....

❖ **Do** go to the parents' evenings at school to find out what your child is going to be studying over the coming term. That way when you ask what homework your offspring has, you won't be fooled into believing that it involves watching the football on telly in order to discuss it the following morning.

....

❖ **Do** try to keep up with the 'new' methods that are being used in school, for example, for teaching maths. Otherwise, when you try to check the homework, you won't have a clue what's going on.

....

❖ **Don't** be tempted to 'help' by re-doing some of the homework questions after your child has gone to bed. It's embarrassing when you still get it wrong; mortifying when it turns out to have been right in the first place.

....

Question: *Why did Mummy say that big yellow book has never been red?*

Answer: 'What she actually said was that the big yellow book had never been "read".'

       'I know, I heard her.'

       'No . . . "read" is different from "red".'

       'No it's not, it's just different from yellow.'

This exchange could go on for hours . . .

Question: *What planet is Australia on?*

Answer: It may be that this child heard someone say something about Australians living on a different planet from the rest of us. There's no point in trying to explain that the turn of phrase that was used by someone suggesting the Australian outlook to life is different from our own. In Australia, after all, they have strange alien creatures like giant mice that hop around on two legs, bears that keep their babies in their pockets and a thing like a mole with the face of a duck. Those things certainly sound like they come from a different planet. Why not throw another spanner in the works and say that Australia isn't on a different planet, it's just out of this world.

Question: *How do you know when you've finally got to sleep?*

Answer: The best answer is a good old dads' joke – lie on the edge of your bed and you'll know straight away if you drop off.

Question: *Could a shark fight a lion?*

Answer: Where is this fight taking place? Lions are actually quite good swimmers, but it's not something that they normally do unless they have to. They can't really deploy their main weapons – claws and teeth – while they are concentrating on swimming and since they've never really learned to use spear guns, they don't have anything to fight with. A lion is also pretty useless underwater because they just can't get wet suits to fit them. A shark, on the other hand, is perfectly at home in the water and could easily bite chunks off a lion as it swam past.

If this battle was to take place on dry land, however, on the grasslands that are the lion's home, the shark would clearly be at a disadvantage. Sharks are great swimmers but, having no legs, they are rubbish at running. Out of the water, of course, they can't breathe, so all the lion would have to do is sit back and watch the shark die. In the water a shark could fight a lion, but on dry land it wouldn't stand a chance.

Question: *What is wood made of?*

Answer: Wood is made of trees. That simple answer is guaranteed, sooner or later, to solicit the response, 'So what are trees made of?' Now is your chance to show off your understanding of 'green' issues. One of the reasons that we need to save the rainforests and plant more trees everywhere is because trees breathe the air and remove carbon from the atmosphere. The carbon is what a tree's wood is made of.

To a child, it might then seem logical to ask, 'But I breathe air, too. Why am I not made of wood?' You can now embark on a long and complicated explanation about how trees absorb carbon dioxide from the air that they breathe in, and breathe out oxygen, while we absorb the oxygen and breathe out carbon dioxide.

On the other hand, for a couple of years you might get away with the simple circular responses, 'Wood is made of trees', and 'Trees are made of wood.'

Question: *Can a policeman arrest a badger?*

Answer: Clearly, if the policeman caught the badger speeding in his Ferrari or attempting to steal the Crown Jewels from the Tower of London, then he could arrest him. As long as the badger doesn't break any laws, however, he can't be arrested.

Question: *Why is a shopping trolley called a trolley?*

Answer: Of course, you could explain that a trolley is simply some kind of cart that runs on wheels. Maintaining that a trolley is just a cart, however, isn't the kind of explanation that will take up much of the journey home from the supermarket. So why not bring your own imagination into play instead?

Clearly, the thin metal from which shopping trolleys are made has to come from somewhere, doesn't it? The mines where such long, thin metal is found are deep underground and, traditionally, the only people who could work in such deep mines were . . . trolls. It's called a trolley because the metal used to make it is mined by trolls. That will either induce a thoughtful silence or start a lively debate that will last all the way home.

Question: *Why does cheese smell so cheesy?*

Answer: Here we have one of the body's best defence mechanisms at work. When it comes to food, the things that smell bad are generally not good to eat. Eating food that has gone bad, or things that have started to go rotten, will make you ill. Your nose gives anything that you are about to eat a good sniff, then passes an emergency message to your brain. The quickest way for your brain to stop your hand moving towards your face and to snap your mouth shut is for it to put out a full body alert that goes, 'Eurgh! Yuk! No!'

You have now given your offspring the excuse never to eat cheese again, so you need to remind them that nobody can be right all the time and your nose sometimes gets it wrong, too. The oleander plant, for example, can smell sweet, some say like bubblegum or sometimes like chocolate, yet it is also one of the most poisonous plants in the world. And if you refuse to eat cheese, you can never have pizza.

Question: *Why is milk white?*

Answer: Well it isn't always, is it? Banana milk is yellow, strawberry milk is pink. The colour of basic milk, of course, is white. Or is it? You could argue that white isn't really a colour at all – it's every colour. The reason that milk appears white is because the tiny particles of the milk emulsion reflect the entire spectrum of natural light. Natural white light, which is made up of all the colours of the rainbow, reflects completely off the emulsion particles, making the milk appear white. That's not really a particularly easy concept for a child to grasp, so maybe you could just try, 'Well, if it was orange your Rice Krispies would look like sick.'

Question: *How soon will I learn to be patient?*

Answer: Wait a minute . . .

Language difficulties

When his wife Leone went back to work following the birth of their second child, Jack, Mark had a bit of a problem to sort out. Little Jack was now a toddler and a real chatterbox who picked up words quite quickly and was beginning to build an impressive vocabulary. He had been attending a day nursery and, for the first couple of weeks of her new job, Leone would be unable either to deliver him to the nursery or to pick him up. She could take their other child, Lara, to school and pick her up at the end of the day, but couldn't do both.

As a dutiful dad, Mark arranged with his boss to work flexible hours that allowed him both to deliver and collect Jack. After two weeks, Mark and Leone would be able to swap duties, which would better suit them both.

Mark's journey to the nursery with Jack involved using a busy stretch of dual carriageway which was the quickest route from their home to Jack's nursery. All went well and after two weeks, Leone took over the nursery run with Jack, while Dad took Lara to school.

Driving along the dual carriageway on the way home one evening, with Jack strapped safely in his child seat in the back of the car, another driver cut in front of Leone, forcing her to brake suddenly. And Jack's voice bawled at the other driver from the back seat, '****HOLE!!'

There was only one place Jack could have picked up this new word and Dad later had to admit that he may have let slip on the dual carriageway once or twice . . .

Question: *Why can't I have more pocket money?*

Answer: The simple answer to this is that if everyone was to give their kids more pocket money whenever they asked for it, then everyone would have to demand more money from their bosses. The boss, suddenly faced with a huge increase in staff wages, would find that his company was in serious trouble and would have to borrow money from the bank. Naturally, he wouldn't be able to pay it all back and neither would the millions of other bosses around the world who had been forced to do the same.

All of the banks would then be in a bad way because they would start to run out of money, so when Dad goes to the 'hole-in-the-wall' to get some cash to give away as pocket money, there is nothing in the machine. Not only that, but the entire banking system would be left in a terrible state. Governments around the world would have to take control to avoid total economic meltdown, with businesses failing and millions of people losing their jobs. And all because some kids thought they deserved more pocket money.

> '*Being a father, being a friend, those are the things that make me feel successful.*'
> WILLIAM HURT

Question: *Why is there no ham in a hamster?*

Answer: The word hamster comes from an old German word 'hamstem' meaning 'to store' and refers to the way that hamsters pack their pouches with food that they store until they need it. In that sense, it has nothing to do with ham meat where the word ham refers to the part of the leg (usually of the pig) from where the meat has been taken.

My father when I was . . .

4 years old: *My daddy can do anything.*
5 years old: *My daddy knows a whole lot.*
6 years old: *My dad is smarter than your dad.*
8 years old: *My dad doesn't know exactly everything.*
10 years old: *In the olden days when my dad grew up, things were different.*
12 years old: *Oh, well, naturally, my father doesn't know anything about that. He is too old to remember his childhood.*
14 years old: *Don't pay attention to my father. He is so old-fashioned!*
21 years old: *Him? He's hopelessly out-of-date.*
25 years old: *Dad knows a little bit about it, but then he should because he has been around so long.*
30 years old: *Maybe we should ask Dad what he thinks. After all, he's had a lot of experience.*
35 years old: *I'm not doing a single thing until I talk to Dad.*
40 years old: *I wonder how Dad would have handled it. He was so wise and had a world of experience.*
50 years old: *I'd give anything if Dad were here now so I could talk this over with him. Too bad I didn't appreciate how smart he was. I could have learned a lot from him.*

ANONYMOUS

What every dad wants

••

EVERY DAD WANTS a hug, of course, but they're not easy to wrap, and they're usually available all year round, not just for Father's Day, birthdays or Christmas. Dads shouldn't only be given hugs on special occasions; they should be given hugs just because they deserve them. That, of course, leaves us no closer to finding the perfect gift for Dad. What *do* dads want?

Most fathers would be appalled if they thought that their kids had spent a fortune buying a gift for them. Small gifts will generally be best, provided that they are thoughtfully chosen and show how much you care, but you have to make sure that the presents fits the dad – and we're not simply talking about buying that 'World's Greatest Dad' t-shirt in XL rather than L. Dads are not all the same. They do like different things.

Buying a bottle of whisky for a teetotaler or a computer game for a technophobe is about as much use as buying a comb for a slaphead or a mirror for Stevie Wonder.

The best gift that you can give a dad is really the same as the best gift that he can give to you – simply be there and try to make the time that you spend with him really special.

'I'm not going to have a better day, a more magical moment, than the first time I heard my daughter giggle.'
SEAN PENN

Top ten Hollywood dads

The legend	The offspring
1. Charlie Chaplin	Eleven children – Norman Spencer Chaplin (who sadly died after only three days), Charles Spencer Chaplin Jr, Sydney Earle, Geraldine Leigh, Michael John, Josephine Hannah, Victoria, Eugene Anthony, Jane Cecil, Annette Emily and Christopher James
2. Mel Gibson	Eight children – Hannah, twins Edward and Christian, William, Louis, Milo, Thomas and Lucia
3. Brad Pitt	Six children – Maddox Chivan (adopted), Pax Thien (adopted), Zahara Marley (adopted), Shiloh Nouvel, and twins Knox Leon and Vivienne Marcheline
4. Dustin Hoffman	Six children – Karina (adopted), Jenna, Jacob Edward, Rebecca, Maxwell Geoffrey and Alexandra Lydia

5. Kevin Costner	Six children – Annie, Lily, Joe, Liam, Hayes and Cayden Wyatt
6. Jack Nicholson	Six children – Jennifer, Honey, Lorraine, Raymond, Caleb and an unidentified daughter with former waitress Jennine Gourin
7. Harrison Ford	Five children – Benjamin, Willard, Malcolm, Georgia and Liam (adopted)
8. Robert de Niro	Five children – Dreena (adopted), Raphael, twins Aaron Kendrick and Julian Henry, and Elliott
9. Sylvester Stallone	Five children – Sage, Seargeoh, Sophie, Sistine and Scarlet. Note how they all begin with 'S'!
10. Arnold Schwarzenegger	Four children – Katherine Eunice, Christina Maria Aurelia, Patrick and Christopher Sargant Shriver

Too cool for words

Sharing special moments with your dad isn't always easy. For most kids there comes a time when it's just not cool to be seen hanging out with their parents. And dads can really struggle when they try to do anything that is even remotely cool. Some kids, however, are lucky enough to have fathers who regularly do the coolest things without any prompting whatsoever.

Bruce Springsteen had a bit of a problem with his dad, Douglas, who was at various times a prison guard, bus driver and factory worker. Douglas wanted a better life for his son, hoping that young Bruce might become a lawyer. The two were never to agree about Bruce's choice of career, but Bruce certainly doesn't have the same problem with his own eldest son, Evan. Unsurprisingly, Evan is also a great rock music fan. 'My son likes a lot of guitar bands,' said Bruce. 'He gave me something the other day which was really good. He'll burn a CD for me full of things that he has, so he's a pretty good call if I want to check out some of that stuff.'

Along with the rest of Bruce's family, Evan, now twenty years old, has appeared on stage with Bruce's E Street Band, playing guitar and singing with his Dad at the Camp Nou Stadium in Barcelona in 2008 in front of more than seventy thousand people. Talk about being seen hanging out with your dad – how cool is that?

The best gift ever

Sonia was struggling to find a Christmas gift for her father. She was heavily pregnant and had been finding the whole experience utterly exhausting. With her husband, David, working all hours to try to ensure that he was on top of everything before the baby arrived, Sonia knew that the preparations for Christmas had to be her responsibility.

For the first time in her life she had shunned the shops in the run up to Christmas, ordering presents online because even the thought of dragging herself round the usual stores left her feeling drained. By Christmas Eve she still hadn't found the right gift for her poor old dad, George.

Since George had retired, he had become something of a gadget geek, joining the legions of 'Silver Surfers' keeping in touch with friends via email, using the Internet with far greater ease than Sonia, and downloading 'apps' for his iPhone that showed him everything from the latest football scores to on-screen star maps of wherever he pointed his phone at the sky.

'To tell the truth,' said Sonia, 'I was a bit jealous of the way that he was able to tune in to all that technology when I don't have a clue about most of it. I'd been trying to find a present for him that he would like, but I really didn't have a clue. David eventually brought home a nice bottle of brandy for him that we planned to give to him at the family gathering on Christmas Day.'

But Sonia and David were destined not to make it to the traditional family Christmas dinner. Late on Christmas Eve, George's phone beeped. There was a message that simply said, 'Dad – couldn't think of what to get you for Christmas. Will this do?' There followed a photograph of a newborn baby with the message, 'Merry Christmas, Grandad, love from George.'

Dos and don'ts for dads: on the beach

❖ **Do** spend ages digging a pool to paddle in, even though the sea is lapping at your ankles.

❖ **Do** go out on that pedalo, even if you are hungover and feeling seasick.

❖ **Do** allow yourself to be buried up to your neck in sand, even if you've just washed the last lot off.

❖ **Don't** be tempted to whip off your trunks and run into the sea on the 'clothing optional' section of the beach for a laugh. The kids will only have buried your trunks by the time you get back . . . for a laugh.

• •

❖ **Don't** work the lobster look. Cooking yourself to a glowing pinky red might seem like a way to work up a manly outdoors look, but you'll be in agony by the end of the day, possibly causing long-term damage to your skin, and setting a bad example to your kids, who need to learn the risks of sun exposure as early as possible.

• •

The sky's the limit

The sky's the limit – that's what Kate thought when she arranged a spectacular sixtieth birthday present for her dad. With her father having lived in Kent, England, all of his life, Kate decided to give him a bird's-eye view of his home county from the basket of a hot air balloon.

The day of the big event came not on his actual birthday but on a late summer afternoon. The sky was clear and conditions were perfect for the balloon ride. Kate was to accompany her dad, along with the balloon pilot, of course, and with much roaring from the burner, they watched the massive red-white-and-blue balloon being inflated until it stood tall and proud above the balloon basket.

When all was ready, Kate and her dad were helped into the basket ready for take-off. With a few more blasts from the burner, the basket left the take-off field as the balloon lifted lazily into the air, revealing spectacular views over the countryside that is often referred to as 'The Garden of England'.

'Dad just said, "Fantastic" and was loving every second of it,' Kate recalled, 'but I looked out of the basket and felt a sudden dread. I heard this sort of primal groaning noise, then realized it was coming from me . . .'

Kate sank down into the bottom of the basket, scared stiff, refusing to look over the edge. 'I'm perfectly okay on aeroplanes,' she said, 'but there was something about the basket being open – and there were no wings or engines.' She huddled in the basket, risking a glance over the edge now and again when her delighted dad, loving every second of it, called out things like, 'Look, there's a great view of Leeds Castle from up here!'

The sky was the limit for Dad's birthday present, but Kate would rather have kept her feet firmly on the ground.

'I felt something impossible for me to explain in words. Then, when they took her away, it hit me. I got scared all over again and began to feel giddy. Then it came to me . . . I was a father.'
NAT KING COLE

Not what Dad wants

It's not just Dad's birthday that can be a problem. Sometimes his best laid plans for his child's birthday treat can go seriously wrong. When Cherie Blair, wife of the former British Prime Minister Tony Blair, was taken out to a posh restaurant on her birthday, things didn't go entirely to her dad's plan.

Cherie's father, actor and political activist Tony Booth, had separated from her mother when Cherie was very young. He had eventually fostered a long-distance relationship with Cherie, who was brought up in Liverpool with her sister, while he lived and worked in London. Cherie received letters and books through the post, cherishing the copy of *Pride and Prejudice* her father sent to her. By the time Cherie's twenty-first birthday came round in 1975, she was a top law student in London with a glittering career ahead of her and her dad was a very well-known face, having starred in the BBC TV series *Till Death Us Do Part* for the previous ten years.

Tony had taken Cherie out to dinner before, but this evening was special. Cherie was hugely impressed when they walked into a very glamorous French restaurant, somewhere she had never been before, but a place where the staff all seemed to know her dad. They ordered the finest of French food starting, of course, with *Escargot* and drank the best wines in the house. Unfortunately, Cherie was not used to such rich fare and was violently sick, bringing her special twenty-first birthday to a less than glamorous conclusion.

'One of the scary things is that, when you're a kid, you look at your dad as the man who has no fear. When you're an adult, you realize your father had fear, and that you have it, too.'
DAVID DUCHOVNY, US ACTOR

Dads in print

WHETHER YOU'RE A twenty-something or seventy-something dad, whether your kids are pre-school or middle-aged, there are some books about fatherhood that will always warm the heart — and sometimes teach you a few lessons along the way.

Danny the Champion of the World
by Roald Dahl

This is a great book for all the rebel dads out there to read to their kids. It tells the tale of Danny and his dad, who owns a filling station, behind which the pair live in a caravan since Danny's mother died. Danny's dad is also a poacher who hunts pheasants on the grounds of a greedy local landowner, Mr Hazell. Not only has Mr Hazell tried to get the filling station shut down, but he set traps on his land, one of which Danny's father falls into and badly injures his ankle. As Danny's father recovers, he and Danny come up with a ruse to humiliate the wicked Mr Hazell. Do they succeed? Well, the title says it all.

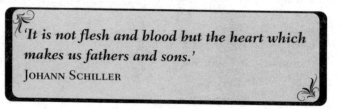

'It is not flesh and blood but the heart which makes us fathers and sons.'
JOHANN SCHILLER

I wanna be like you-oo-oo

At some point in their lives, most boys want to be just like their dads. Following in your father's footsteps is a great idea if your dad can pass on a few tips about the family business, or teach his son the skills required to become a butcher, a carpenter or a plumber. It is far more difficult to emulate your dad if he has what is now often taken to be the most powerful job in the world – President of the United States.

Only two men have ever followed their fathers into the White House. John Adams was America's second President (1797–1801), succeeding George Washington, and was the first President to take up residence in the newly completed White House. Adams' son, John Quincy Adams, had escorted his father on diplomatic missions to Europe prior to Adams senior becoming President. He clearly picked up some of his father's political skill because he became the sixth President of the United States in 1825.

Rolling forward 164 years, George Herbert Walker Bush was elected as the forty-first President of the United States in 1989, succeeding Ronald Reagan. Bill Clinton took over the Presidency in 1993, serving until 2001 when the top job passed back to the Bush family, George Walker Bush holding the post until 2009.

The Swiss Family Robinson
by Johann Wyss

The subtitle of this book is 'Adventures of a father and mother and four sons in a desert island', and what an adventure it is. Led by their father, a Swiss pastor (as Wyss himself was), the Robinson family turn a catastrophic accident at sea into a bold new life on a tropical island. Narrated by Father Robinson himself, the book shows this cavalier man teaching his kids by example, demonstrating bravery, remarkable knowledge of tropical plants and animals, and of course age-old wisdom. Mother Robinson's clearly his perfect match, whipping up a vegetable garden in no time. This is the family all of us wish we could be a part of.

To Kill a Mockingbird
by Harper Lee

What child reading this didn't wish their dad was Atticus Finch, and what dad didn't hope that he could be one tenth as manly? Scout Finch, the six-year-old narrator, tells the story of growing up in Alabama in Depression-era America, with her brother Jem and her widowed father Atticus, a lawyer. As the children play with their new friend Dill and spy on the mysterious Boo Radley, Atticus takes on a case representing an African-American man falsely accused of raping a white woman. Throughout the book, Atticus teaches the children through his words and actions that it is wrong and dangerous to judge others simply because they are different. A real tear-jerker, this one.

'When a child asks you something, answer him, for goodness sake. But don't make a production of it. Children are children, but they can spot an evasion faster than adults, and evasion simply muddles 'em.'
SPOKEN BY ATTICUS FINCH IN *To Kill a Mockingbird* BY HARPER LEE

Man and Boy
by Tony Parsons

This bestselling book is a tale of modern fatherhood, with the novel's protagonist, TV executive Harry Silver (allegedly based on the author himself), left to bring up his son alone after the breakdown of his marriage due to his infidelity. As he also loses his job, Harry is forced to be a stay-at-home dad, and has to face up to the responsibilities he has so far studiously managed to avoid. A touching and honest look at a man having to grow up in order to be a good father.

Life After God
by Douglas Coupland

The full collection of these short stories isn't entirely concerned with being a father, but 'Little Creatures' and more particularly 'Gettysburg' powerfully illustrate the overwhelming emotions of joy, wonder, fear and, ultimately, love, that exist between parent and child. They are a beautiful ode to fatherhood.

Gilead
by Marilynne Robinson

This Pulitzer prize-winning novel set in Iowa, America, takes the form of a letter by seventy-six-year-old Reverend John Ames to his six-year-old son, as Ames nears the end of his life. A meditative summation of his own life, the Reverend's letter is strongly concerned with families, and most particularly fathers and sons; his own father and grandfather had been estranged and unable to resolve their differences, despite their love for each other. Ultimately, the book emphasizes the importance of families, ancestors, and the messages we pass down from generation to generation.

> *'Certain is it that there is no kind of affection so purely angelic as of a father to a daughter. In love to our wives there is desire; to our sons, ambition; but to our daughters there is something which there are no words to express.'*
> JOSEPH ADDISON

The *Harry Potter* books
by J.K.Rowling

Harry wouldn't have his incredible wizardly talents were it not for his father James. Like Harry, James was an exceptionally gifted student at Hogwarts School of Witchcraft and Wizardry, where he met Harry's mother, Lily. Sadly the evil Voldemort vows to hunt down the couple in order to destroy Harry, due to a prophecy about their son. Bravely, James tells Lily to take Harry and run while he stays to face Voldemort alone, which means certain death. While Lily also doesn't survive, her and James' bravery in sacrificing themselves means Harry lives to become the hero we all know and love.

> *'One father is worth more than a hundred schoolmasters.'*
> ENGLISH PROVERB

Inherited goods

Few father and son pairings have garnered so much attention and press coverage as the writers Kingsley and Martin Amis. Both renowned for their love of the high life and for their literary talents, they were nevertheless extremely different in their writing styles.

The younger Amis felt his lauded father's credentials in fact worked against him in his own career, since he felt his famous name caused a degree of resentment amongst literary critics. He suggests that he is seen as being 'like the son of the lord of the manor who has inherited the estate by right of birth where others have had to struggle. In as much as heredity counts, there might be something in it.' However, Amis Jr does acknowledge his father's huge influence on him. When a reader of the *Independent* newspaper enquired what Martin would have done for a career were his father not a writer, he responded: 'If he had been a postman, then I would have been a postman. If he had been a travel agent, then I would have been a travel agent.'

The Darling Buds of May
by H.E. Bates

Who didn't want to be a member of the Larkin family, with their constant high japes and seemingly endless summers of fun? At the heart of this happy bunch was Pop Larkin, who drank and flirted his way through life in the 1950s English countryside. With their improbably named children – Mariette, Zinnia, Petunia, Primrose, Victoria, and Montgomery – Pop and Ma lived a life of rustic merriment. Pop's liberal and laidback attitude to life saw him encouraging his daughter's blossoming relationship with the tax inspector Cedric 'Charley' Charlton, dealing in junk and generally living a life of rural bliss. As Pop himself said on many occasions, 'It's all perfick.'

> *'The father of a daughter is nothing but a high-class hostage. A father turns a stony face to his sons, berates them, shakes his antlers, paws the ground, snorts, runs them off into the underbrush, but when his daughter puts her arm over his shoulder and says, "Daddy, I need to ask you something," he is a pat of butter in a hot frying pan.'*
> GARRISON KEILLOR

A Father's worst fears!

Dear Dad,

It is with a heavy heart that I write this letter.

I decided to elope with my new girlfriend Tamara. We wanted to avoid a scene with you and Mum.

I've found real passion with Tamara and she is so lovely – even with her nose piercing, tattoos, and her tight motorcycle clothes. But it's not only the joy, Dad – she's pregnant and Tamara said that we will be very happy.

Even though you won't care for her as she is so much older than me, she already owns a trailer in the woods and has a stack of firewood for the whole winter. She wants to have many more children with me and that's now one of my dreams too.

Tamara taught me that marijuana doesn't really hurt anyone, and we'll be growing it for us and trading it with her friends for all the drugs we want!

Don't worry Dad, I'm fifteen years old now and I know how to take care of myself. Someday I'm sure we'll be back to visit, so you can get to know your grandchildren

Your ever loving son,

Eddie.

PS: Don't worry Dad, none of the above is true. I'm over at next door's house. I just wanted to remind you that there are worse things in life than my end of year school report, which is in the centre drawer of my desk. I love you!

PPS: Call when it is safe for me to come home.

Dreams from My Father
by Barack Obama

While this is the autobiography of Barack Obama's early life up to his years at Harvard Law School, it is also a reflective and emotional book about the influence of father on son, even when he is mostly absent from his life. Obama jokes, 'I've been sent by my father from the planet Krypton to save the Earth', and in his subsequent rise to the American presidency, it seems his dad really did father a Superman for our times.

What makes dads so great

SO YOU'VE HEARD from dads famous, historical and real-life, you've learned to distinguish your dos from your don'ts, discovered more ways to have fun with the kids, learned how to deflect those tricky questions the little tykes throw at you, groaned at the (all too familiar) dad jokes, and gone misty-eyed at the tales of various fathers' derring-do. What better way to conclude this celebration of Dad than by summarizing what makes him so great in the first place?

He might always answer the phone with the phrase 'I'll just get your mum', he may seemingly spend most of our teenage years on a single-minded mission to cause us as much embarrassment as humanly possible, and he might still mix our name up with our siblings'. But like the Scarlet Pimpernel and Clark Kent before him, underneath his apparently bumbling exterior, Dad is a one-man world-saving superhero, with a superhuman knowledge of bikes, sheds and bad jokes.

Let's face it, you could fill an entire book with what exactly it is that makes Dad so great, but here are some final thoughts that really capture what it is that makes us say *I Love You, Dad*.

❖ He won't mind if you make a mess.

❖ He scares away awful boyfriends/girlfriends.

❖ He puts family first.

❖ Even the shortest walk becomes an adventure with him.

❖ He has lousy fashion sense but his music collection's surprisingly good.

> *'Problem with the car? Confusion over the house insurance? Need to put up a shelf? I'll call my Dad.'*
> DAVID TENNANT

Top ten rockin' dads

Rock God	Offspring
1. Bruce Springsteen	Evan James, Jessica Rae, Sam Ryan
2. Rod Stewart	Sarah, Kimberley, Sean, Ruby, Renee, Liam, Alastair
3. Ozzy Osbourne	Elliot (adopted), Jessica, Louis, Aimee, Kelly, Jack, Robert (adopted)
4. Mick Jagger	Karis, Jade, Elizabeth, James, Georgia, Gabriel, Lucas
5. Paul McCartney	Heather (adopted), Mary, Stella, James, Beatrice
6. Stevie Wonder	Aisha, Keita, Kwame, Mumtaz, Sophia, Kailand, Mandla
7. Sting	Joseph, Fuchsia, Bridget, Jake, Eliot, Pauline
8. Roger Taylor	Felix Luther, Rory Eleanor, Rufus Tiger, Tiger Lily, Lola May

9. Bob Dylan	Maria (adopted), Jesse, Anna, Samuel, Jakob, Desiree
10. David Gilmour	Alice, Clare, Sara, Matthew, Charlie (adopted), Joe, Gabriel, Romany

> *'Any man can be a father. It takes someone special to be a dad.'*
> ANON

❖ He lets you make your own mistakes . . .

❖ . . . but says 'no' when you need to hear it.

❖ You know he'd protect you if you were in danger.

❖ He makes you laugh, although usually unintentionally.

❖ Whether you're four years old or forty, you know he'll still be there for you.

❖ You spend your childhood thinking he's Clint Eastwood, Bruce Lee and Michael Schumacher all rolled into one.

❖ He tells great stories of his own childhood – which get more fantastical the older he gets.

❖ He doesn't mind getting his hands dirty – in fact, he enjoys it.

❖ He's just a big kid himself.

Acknowledgements

Many thanks to Louise Dixon and Hannah Knowles at Michael O'Mara Books for all their help in making this book happen. Thanks also to Kay Hayden for her excellent design work.